Brain Teasers

TOP THAT

Licensed exclusively to Top That Publishing Ltd
Tide Mill Way, Woodbridge, Suffolk, IP12 1AP, UK
www.topthatpublishing.com
Copyright © 2016 Tide Mill Media
All rights reserved
0 2 4 6 8 9 7 5 3 1
Manufactured in Zhejiang, China

1. Triangle Tangle

This triangle is constructed from 10 coins. What is the smallest number of coins that need to be moved to make the triangle point downward?

2. Mind Teaser

What is yours to own, yet others use it more?

3. Word Play

Change one letter from the existing words below to create a new word.

Change FISH to a plate you eat off.   _ ISH

Change GOOD to a forest of trees.   _ OOD

Change TOW to the opposite of high.   _ OW

4. Number Hunt

Three numbers between 1-30 are missing from the box. Can you find out which ones are missing?

30   14   29   23
10   19
11   22
27   15   12
2
21
3   7
5
8
25   18
17   6   4
20
26   24
1   13

5. Anagram Antics

Unscramble each of these words to find something in the picture.

TARPIE

RATE SURE

GALF JLLOY RROGE

DWORS

6. Riddling Remark

What happens only in the middle of each month,
and happens only in the night, never in the day?

7. Baffling Birthday

Megan was born on December 27, yet her birthday always falls in the summer. How is this possible?

8. Super Sequence

Guess what the next two numbers will be. See if you can spot what is special about the number sequence.

7

14

17

21

27

28

35

37

_ ?

_ ?

9. Hot Dilemma

A man is trapped in a room. The room only has two doors through which to escape. Through the first door is a glass room and the heat from the sun instantly fries anyone who enters. Through the second door is a fire-breathing dragon. How does the man escape?

10. Running Riddle

What can run but never walks, has a mouth but never talks, has a head but never weeps, and has a bed but never sleeps?

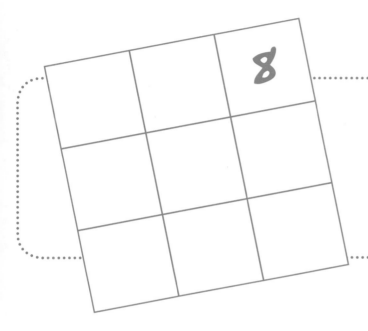

11. Bewilder Box

Fill in the numbers 1 to 9, so that every row, column and diagonal adds up to 15. You can use each number only once!

12. Film Frolics

James watched a movie on TV. The movie lasted 2 hours and 5 minutes. It finished at 23:00. What time did the movie start?

13. Letter Enigma

Fill in the missing letters to solve the clues.

You go here to learn.   _ _ _ OOL

Sheep keep warm with this.   _ OOL

The opposite of warm.   _ OOL

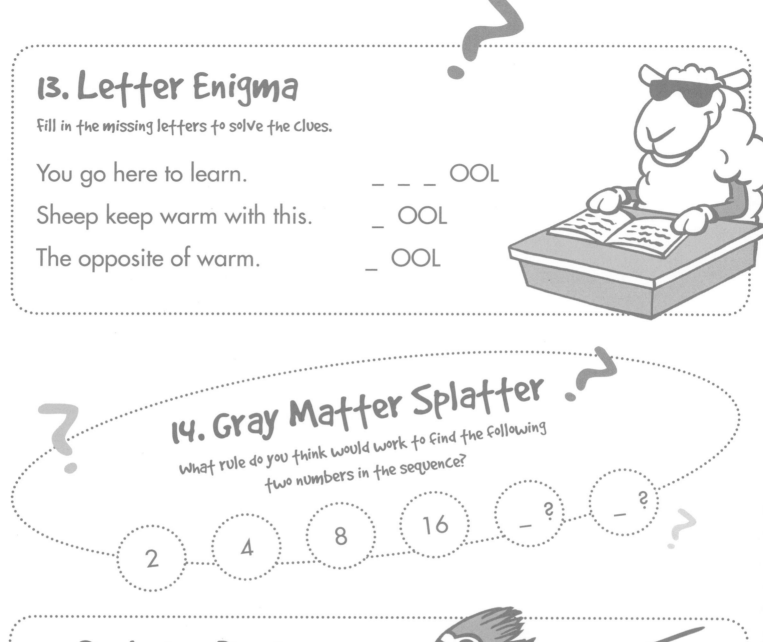

14. Gray Matter Splatter

What rule do you think would work to find the following two numbers in the sequence?

2   4   8   16   _ ?   _ ?

15. Rock the Boat

Two girls want to cross a river. The only way to get to the other side is by boat, but that boat can only take one girl at a time. The boat cannot return on its own but both girls manage to cross to the other side. How did they do it?

16. Odd One Out

One number here is the odd one out. Can you figure out why?

5, 16, 20, 25, 50

17. Tricky Thinking

What has a face and two hands but no arms or legs?

18. Say What You See

What nautical term does this represent?

man

———

board

19. What Am I?

I have holes in my top and bottom, my left and right and in the middle, but I still hold water. What am I?

20. Letter Assembler

Rearrange the letters below to make a nine-letter word that means something is funny.

LAHOURISI

21. What Can it Be?

What does this represent?

SEGG

GESG

EGSG

Clue: think about what chickens lay!

22. Mix and Match

Pair up the words which go best together.

cow
horse
rabbit
dog
chicken
pig

hutch
egg
trotters
saddle
milk
lead

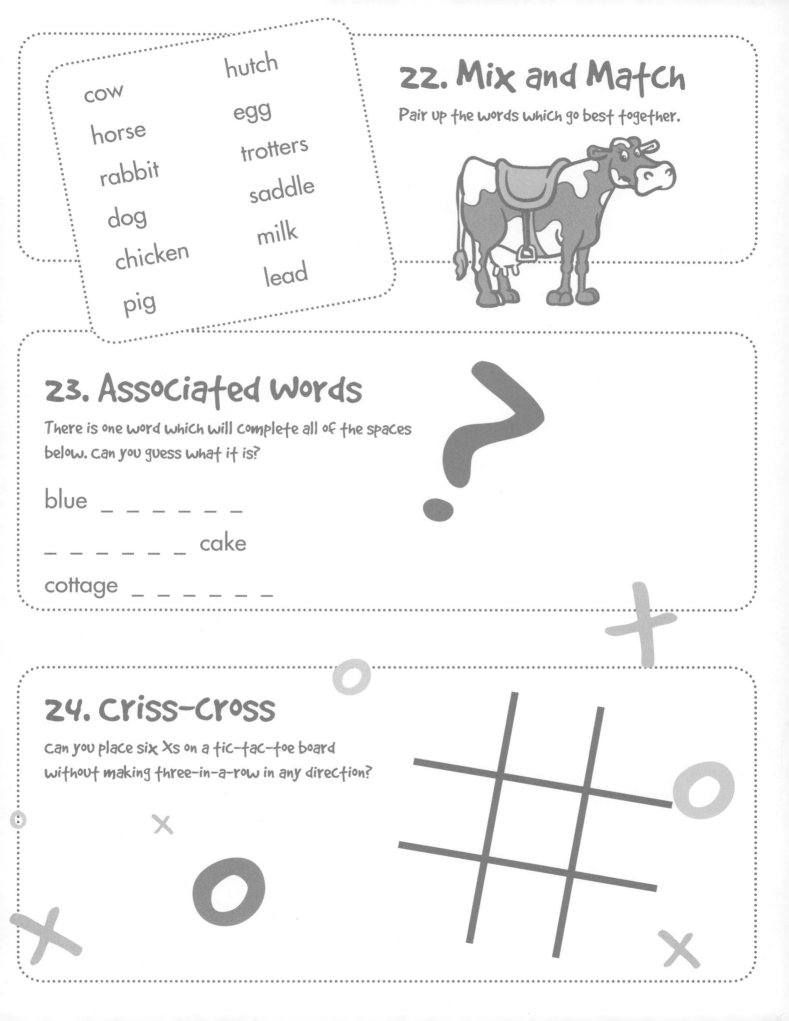

23. Associated Words

There is one word which will complete all of the spaces below. Can you guess what it is?

blue _ _ _ _ _ _ _

_ _ _ _ _ _ _ cake

cottage _ _ _ _ _ _

24. Criss-Cross

Can you place six Xs on a tic-tac-toe board without making three-in-a-row in any direction?

25. Dotty Difficulty

Nine dots are arranged in a three by three square. Connect each of the nine dots using only four straight lines and without lifting your pen off the paper.

26. Solve It!

What can you catch but cannot throw?

27. Proverb Puzzle

Rearrange the letters to form a well-known saying. There are five letters in the first word of the answer, three letters in the second, four letters in the third and three letters in the fourth.

SWAT ON A TOWN TENT

28. Guessing Game

The day before yesterday I was 15 and next year I will be 18. This is true only one day in a year.

What day is my birthday?

29. Read the Signs

What mathematical symbol can be placed between 5 and 9, to get a number greater than 5 and smaller than 9?

30. Hop to It!

Two mothers and two daughters go to a pet store and buy three rabbits. Each female gets her own rabbit. How is this possible?

31. Back Word

What word, when written in capital letters, is the same forward, backward and upside down?

Clue: think about a time of day.

32. Letter Logic

In each of these words, change the underlined letter to produce five new words. The new letters will spell a fruit. Can you work it out?

D<u>A</u>TE

N<u>U</u>T

<u>L</u>IME

P<u>E</u>ACH

<u>P</u>EAR

33. Word Wizard

Can you find the nine-letter word that begins and ends with vowels? Each letter can only be used once!

C

R

O

E

H

S

R

A

T

34. Ticking clock

Jim looks into a mirror and sees the clock reflecting the time behind him. It appears to be 2.30 pm. Jim thinks he is really late! What time is it really?

35. Racing Riddle

You are in a race and you overtake the person who is in second place. What position are you in now?

36. Cryptic Countries

Discover the missing words and uncover the missing countries. Answer the country clues by rhyming with the first answer you gave. Use the hints to help! All the countries end in "land."

Something you would put a plant in.

_ _ _

+

The men from this country wear kilts.

= S _ _ _ _ LAND

A way of cooking food in a pan.

_ _ _

+

A country of temples and elephants.

= T _ _ _ _ LAND

You roll them in board games.

_ _ _ _

+

Lots of snow and cold weather here!

= I _ _ LAND

37. Ball Games

Becca is by herself. She throws a ball as hard as she can and it comes back to her without bouncing off anything. There is nothing attached to it, and no one else catches or throws it back. How does Becca get the ball back?

38. Missing Alphabet

Find the two letters missing from the ball.

?

39. Enigma

Answer the clues, then create a new word by joining the two answers together.

wet weather + a ribbon in the hair = ?

40. Let's Celebrate!

What word can be put before all the words below?
These things may all be linked to a special occasion!

_____ cake

_____ ring

_____ dress

_____ day

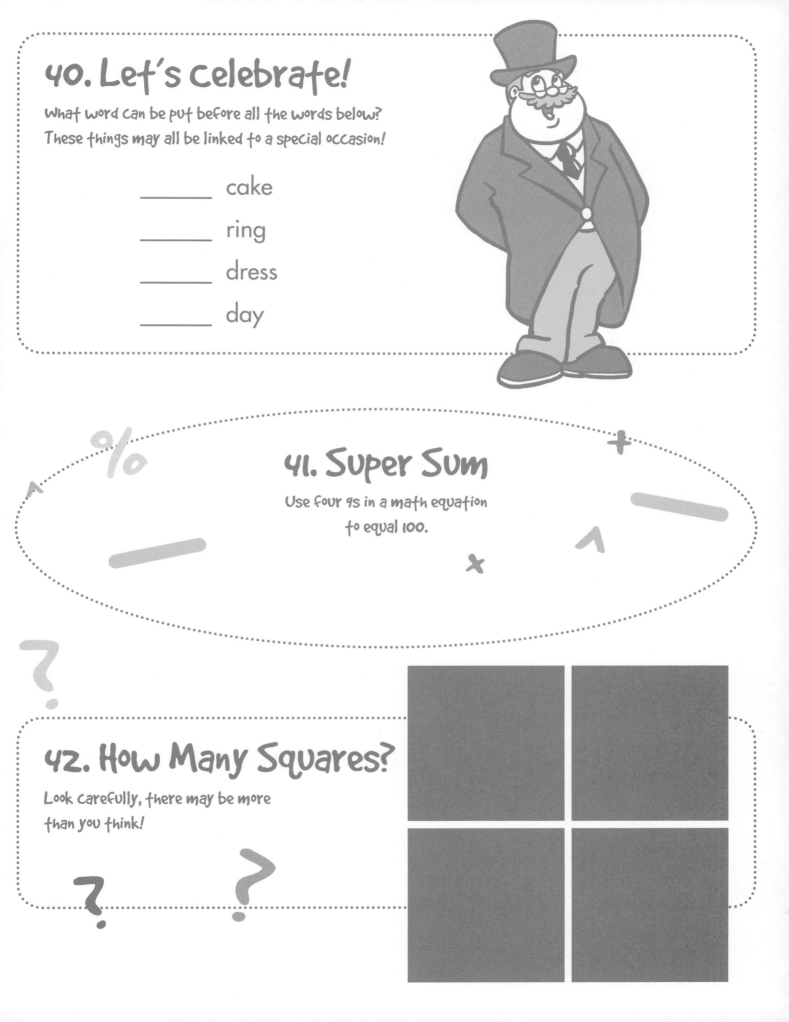

41. Super Sum

Use four 9s in a math equation
to equal 100.

42. How Many Squares?

Look carefully, there may be more
than you think!

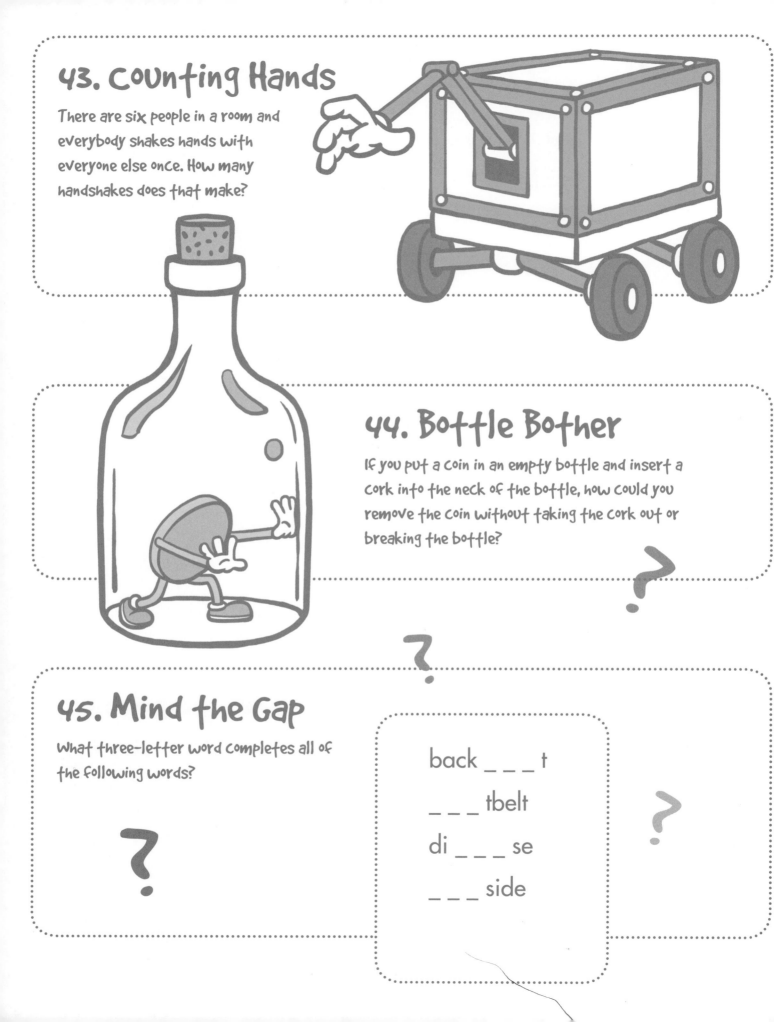

43. Counting Hands

There are six people in a room and everybody shakes hands with everyone else once. How many handshakes does that make?

44. Bottle Bother

If you put a coin in an empty bottle and insert a cork into the neck of the bottle, how could you remove the coin without taking the cork out or breaking the bottle?

45. Mind the Gap

What three-letter word completes all of the following words?

back _ _ _ t

_ _ _ tbelt

di _ _ _ se

_ _ _ side

46. Animal Antics

Can you name the animals missing from the nursery rhymes?

Itsy bitsy _Spider_

Four little speckled _Mouse_

This little _ _ _ _ _ went to market

Mary had a little _l a m b_

47. Match Mayhem

Match up the pairs with their opposites. Which item is not in a pair?

Window!

cat

window

dog

sunshine

angel

rain cloud

devil

48. Guessing Game

You know even before you depart that you will end back at the start.

It is loopy, and brings out emotions, sometimes it causes a commotion.

It speeds and twists above the ground. It can turn a frown upside down.

What is it?

49. Wordy Fact

What is the only word in the English language that ends in the letters "mt?"

50. Letter Look-See

Unscramble the word below.

EPWERYTIRT

51. Spot It!

What is special about these words below?

race car

kayak

52. Lost Letter

Look at the numbers below. There is one vowel that is never used. Can you see what it is?

One, two, three, four, five, six, seven, eight, nine, ten.

A E I
O U

53. Fishing Fun

If it takes three fishermen three minutes to catch three fish, how many fishermen are needed to catch six fish in six minutes?

54. Lurking Letters

Look at the word below.

THEREIN

This one word contains 10 words without rearranging any of its letters. Can you find them all?

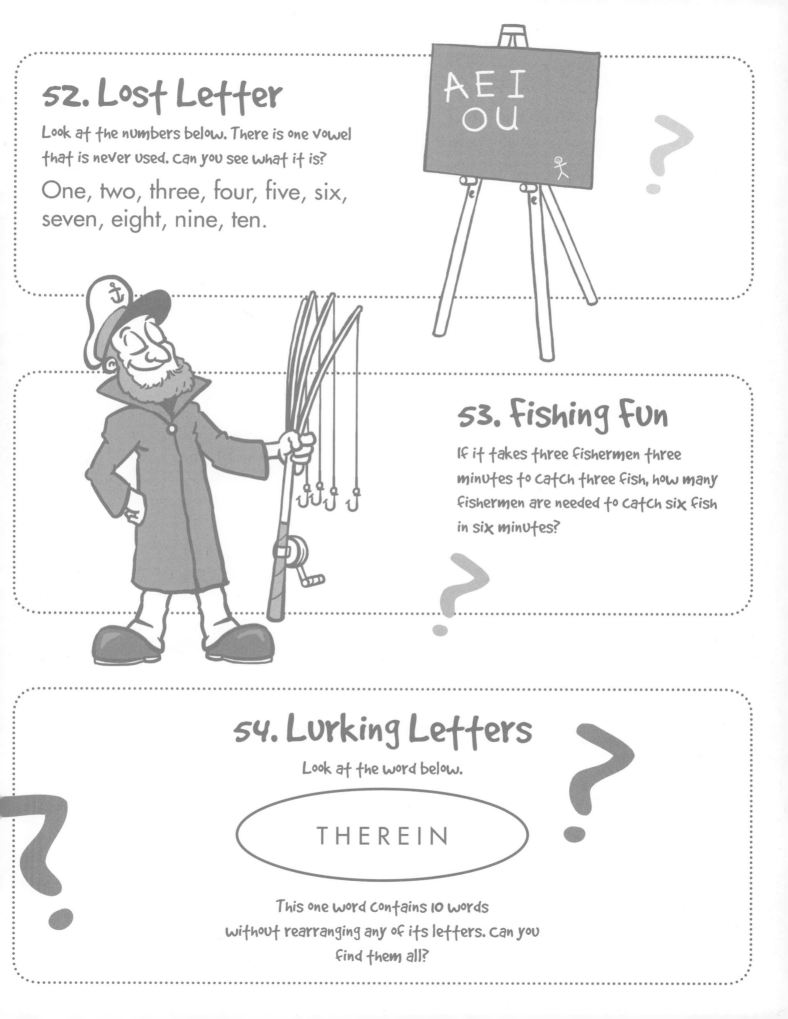

55. What's for Supper?

A visiting alien is trying some delicious human food. To find out exactly what it is, you must complete the sums below.

$12 + 10 =$ _ _ (D)

$20 - 10 =$ _ _ (O)

$9 - 5 =$ _ _ (H)

$15 - 5 =$ _ _ (O)

$3 \times 1 =$ _ _ (T)

$7 \times 2 =$ _ _ (G)

Now copy the letters into the numbered blanks at the bottom of the page to reveal the answer.

_ _ _ / _ _ _

4 10 3   22 10 14

56. Body Trivia

Can you name 10 parts of the body that are spelled with three letters? Start at the top and work your way down.

57. Sneaky Sequence

Each letter is in the right order, but what do they signify?

JFMAMJJASOND

58. Sentence Structure

What does this sentence use all of?

THE QUICK BROWN FOX JUMPS
OVER THE LAZY DOG

59. Family Photo

Can you guess how the speaker is related to the man in the riddle? Who is the man?

"Brothers and sisters I have none but this man's father is my father's son."

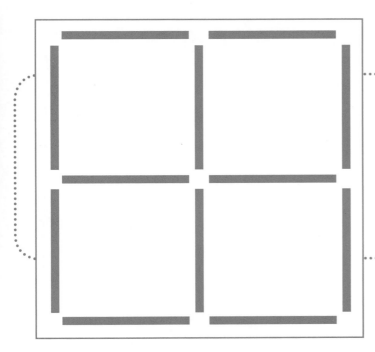

60. Stick Shapes

Can you move just two sticks to create seven squares?

61. Car Caper

A four-wheeled car has traveled 45,000 miles on its four tires. They have not been changed. How far has each separate tire traveled?

62. Guess the Saying

Look at the picture above and say what you see!

63. Calendar Calculus

Some months have 30 days, some months have 31 days. How many have 28?

64. Proverb Palaver

Match the missing words to the correct proverbs to complete the saying.

MINDS

SILVER

APPLE

BIRD

AN _____ A DAY KEEPS THE DOCTOR AWAY.

EVERY CLOUD HAS A _____ LINING.

GREAT _____ THINK ALIKE.

THE EARLY _____ CATCHES THE WORM.

65. Animal Antics

If a rooster sits on the border of Scotland and England, where would the egg drop?

66. Probability Pickle

You have 12 black socks and 12 white socks mixed up in a drawer. You're up early and it's too dark to tell them apart. What is the smallest number of socks you need to take out to be sure of having a matching pair?

67. Number Crunch

Find two numbers in the mix that when multiplied together make a total of 72.

⑤

⑥

⑦

⑨

⑧

68. Absolute Anagrams

This is the name and position of a historical figure from England. Can you unscramble the words below to find out who it is?

EQNEU TIAVICOR

☐☐☐☐☐   ☐☐☐☐☐☐☐☐

69. Look at the Line

Complete this sequence of letters:

O, T, T, F, F, S, S, E, N, _

70. Full House

Claire's mum had five children. They were named February, March, April, May and . . . ?

71. Picture Puzzle

Use the picture to work out what the saying is.

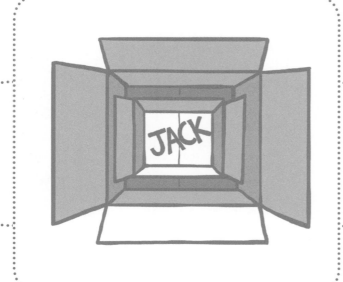

72. Fruit Swap

Chris and Phil both have some apples. If Chris gives Phil an apple, they will both have the same number of apples. However, if Phil gives Chris an apple, Chris will have twice as many as Phil. How many apples do Chris and Phil each have?

73. Magic Trick

Five magicians share out a box of magic wands. The first four magicians each take five wands. The last magician has half the box to himself.

How many wands were there altogether?

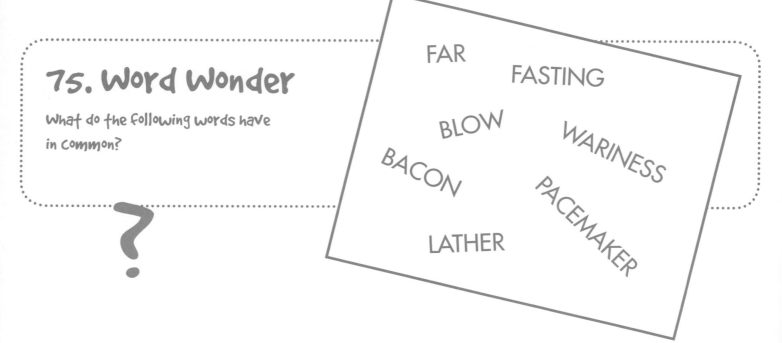

74. Money Malarkey

A dad told his son he would give him 5 cents for every correct answer on his geometry test. His son replied that he would pay 8 cents for every incorrect answer. There were 26 questions on the test but no money was exchanged. Why?

75. Word Wonder

What do the following words have in common?

FAR   FASTING

BLOW   WARINESS

BACON

PACEMAKER

LATHER

76. Anagram Assortment

Place three words in the blank spaces so the sentences make sense. All the missing words are anagrams of each other. Change the letter order in the words to complete the sentence.

LISA _ _ _ HER BISCUITS, BUT
I DIDN'T _ _ _ MINE—I HAD A CUP
OF _ _ _ INSTEAD.

77. Monkey Business

A zebra was going to the river. On the way, the zebra passed five elephants. Each elephant had five monkeys on its neck. How many animals were going to the river?

78. Word Play

What do these words have in common?

BANANA

POTATO

GRAMMAR

DRESSER

79. What Can it Be?

Think hard to find out the answer.

Forward I am heavy, but backward I am not. What am I?

80. Flower Power

Here are some flowers with the vowels removed.
Have a guess at what they are.

VLT

BTTRCP

LLY

TLP

81. Nimble Numbers

How is 7 different from the rest of the
numbers from 1 to 10?

82. Ant Antics

Three ants are traveling in the same direction. The first ant has two ants behind him, the second ant has one in front and one behind, but the third ant has one in front and one behind too.

How is this possible?

83. What Do You See?

Look and guess what the saying is!

1 2 3 S A F E T Y 4 5 6

84. Matchmaker

Pair up the flags to the countries listed below.

Japan

Canada

Greece

A.

B.

C.

85. Raid the fridge

The names of items found in the fridge are hidden in each of the sentences. Find them by taking a letter from each word.

BIRDS USE TWEETS TO ENJOY RADIO

MONKEYS EMPLOY APE TEACHERS

FAIRIES ROAM UNDER INTERESTING TREES

X E Q W B

N P H M

C Z I R U

T S O

V A D

G J K

86. Bug Hunt

The letters missing from this box make up the name of an insect.

Can you name it?

87. Choppy Waters!

The ladder at the back of a fishing boat has 10 steps. The distance between each step is 10 inches. If the waves rise 5 inches every half an hour, how long will it take for six steps to disappear beneath the waves?

88. Smooth Sequence

What are the next two letters in the series?

B, C, D, E, G, P, _ , _ .

89. Rodeo Riddle

A cowboy rode into town on friday, stayed for four days, and rode out again on friday. How did he manage that?

90. Catch of the Day

Two fathers and two sons go fishing. Each of them catches one fish, but they only bring three fish back with them. Why is that?

91. Shady Puzzle

Solve the clues to find an answer that contains six letters.
The letters in the shaded boxes spell the magical word you have to find.

1. Opposite of summer ☐ _ _ _ _ _
2. Princesses usually wed a _ _ ☐ _ _ _
3. Black and white striped African animals ☐ _ _ _ _ _
4. Cows eat it and snakes lie in it _ _ ☐ _ _
5. An optical illusion image in the desert _ _ ☐ _ _ _
6. Move to music ☐ _ _ _ _

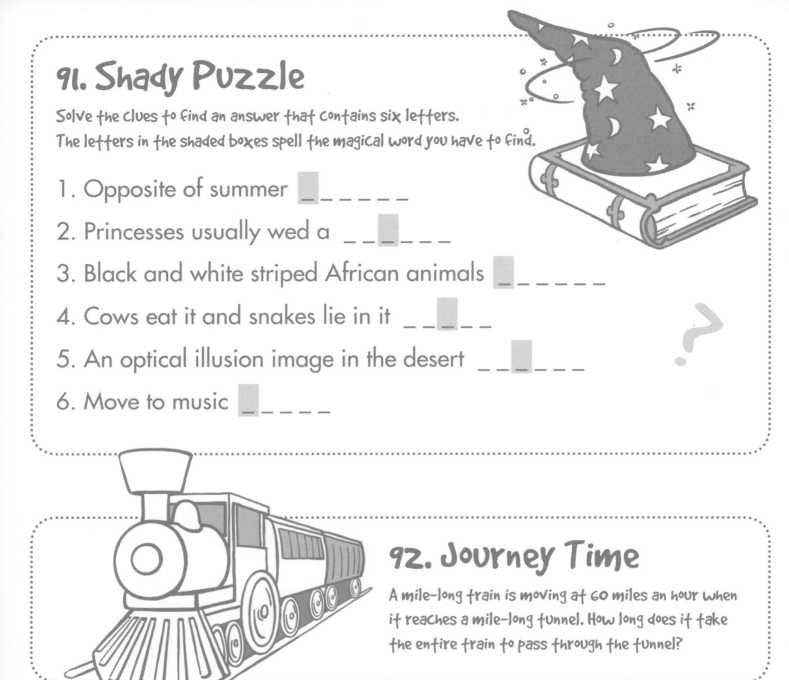

92. Journey Time

A mile-long train is moving at 60 miles an hour when it reaches a mile-long tunnel. How long does it take the entire train to pass through the tunnel?

93. Letter Jumble

All the missing six-letter words are anagrams of each other. Change the letter order in the words to complete the sentence.

LIZ BOUGHT LOTS OF FRUIT. SHE WAS _ _ _ _ _ _ WHEN SHE ATE SOME BITTER _ _ _ _ _ _ , SO SHE ATE THE JUICY _ _ _ _ _ _ INSTEAD.

94. Wriggly Riddle

If a man carried my burden he would break his back. I am not big but leave silver in my tracks. What am I?

95. Wordplay Array

Place three words in the blanks to complete the sentence. All of the missing words are anagrams of each other. Change the letter order in the words to complete the sentence.

THE QUEEN LOOKED _ _ _ _ _ IN HER ROBES. SHE LIKED TO _ _ _ _ _ AT SERVANTS WHILE SHE SAT ON HER _ _ _ _ _ THRONE.

96. Mind Melt

What can be taller than you are and yet does not weigh anything?

97. Number Storm

Find two numbers in the box which, when added together and multiplied by ten, equal 50.

98. Word Mix

Rearrange the letters to spell two buccaneering words.

STAR HIPPIE

99. Flavor Frolics

Here are some ice cream flavors with their vowels removed. Can you guess what they are?

CHCLT   STRWBRRY

VNLL   MNT

100. Guessing Game

What fruity treat does this represent?

BAN ANA

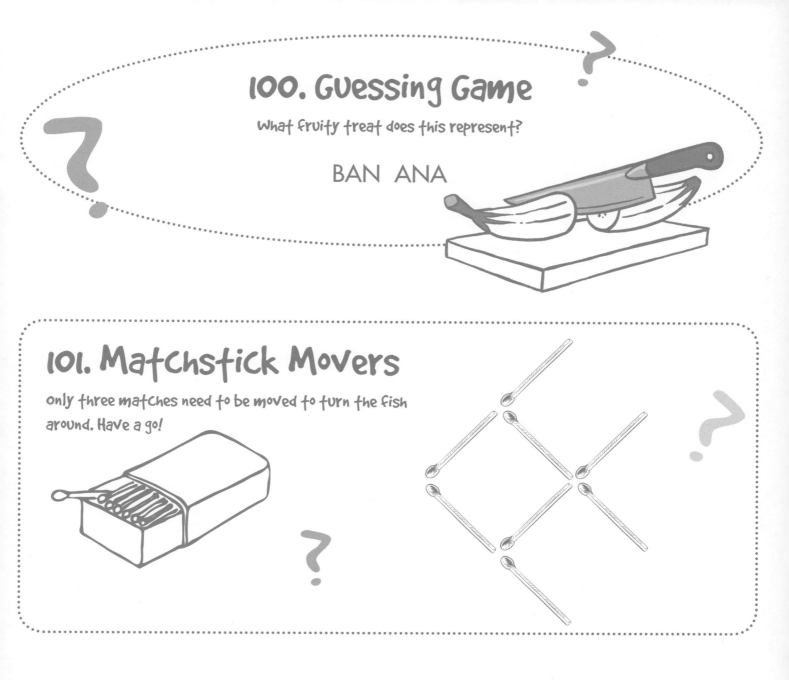

101. Matchstick Movers

Only three matches need to be moved to turn the fish around. Have a go!

ANSWERS

1. Triangle Tangle

3.

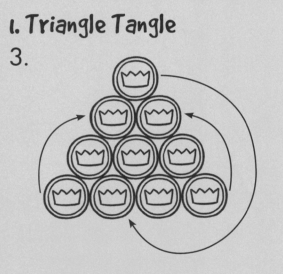

2. Mind Teaser

Your name.

3. Word Play

DISH, WOOD, LOW.

4. Number Hunt

9, 16 and 28 are missing.

5. Anagram Antics

PIRATE, TREASURE, JOLLY
ROGER FLAG, SWORD.

6. Riddling Remark
The letter N.

7. Baffling Birthday
She lives in the Southern Hemisphere.

8. Super Sequence
42, 47—they are the numbers that either contain the digit 7 or are divisible by 7.

9. Hot Dilemma
He waits until nighttime and then goes through the first door.

10. Running Riddle
A river.

11. Bewilder Box

4	3	8
9	5	1
2	7	6

12. Film Frolics
20:55.

13. Letter Enigma
SCHOOL
WOOL
COOL.

14. Gray Matter Splatter
32, 64—multiply each number by 2 to get the next number.

15. Rock the Boat
The girls were standing on the opposite sides of the river.

16. Odd One Out
16 is the odd one out—all the others are multiples of 5.

17. Tricky Thinking
A clock.

18. Say What You See
Man overboard.

19. What Am I?
A sponge.

20. Letter Assembler
HILARIOUS.

21. What Can it Be?
Scrambled eggs.

22. Mix and Match
cow / milk
horse / saddle
rabbit / hutch
dog / lead
chicken / egg
pig / trotters.

23. Associated Words
Cheese.

24. Criss-Cross

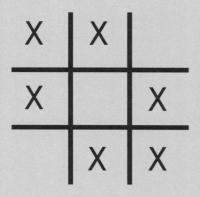

25. Dotty Difficulty

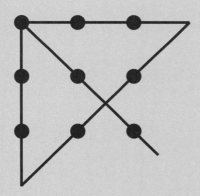

26. Solve It!
A cold.

27. Proverb Puzzle
WASTE NOT WANT NOT.

28. Guessing Game
They were born on December 31 and talked about it on January 1.

29. Read the Signs
A decimal point between 5 and 9.

30. Hop to It!
There is a grandmother, a mother and a daughter.

31. Back Word
NOON.

32. Letter Logic

LATE

NET

MIME

POACH

NEAR

The name of the fruit spelled out is: LEMON.

33. Word Wizard

ORCHESTRA.

34. Ticking Clock

10.30 am.

35. Racing Riddle

Second place.

36. Cryptic Countries

SCOTLAND

THAILAND

ICELAND.

37. Ball Games

Becca threw the ball straight up in the air.

38. Missing Alphabet

F and S.

39. Enigma

Rainbow.

40. Let's Celebrate!
Wedding.

41. Super Sum
99 + (9 divided by 9) = 100.

42. How Many Squares?
5.

43. Counting Hands
15.

44. Bottle Bother
Push the cork into the bottle and shake the coin out.

45. Mind the Gap
Sea.

46. Animal Antics
Spider
Frogs
Piggy
Lamb.

47. Match Mayhem
Window.

48. Guessing Game
A rollercoaster.

49. Wordy Fact
"Dreamt" is the only word in the English language that ends in the letters "mt."

50. Letter Look-See
TYPEWRITER.

51. Spot It!
They are palindromes, which means that they can be read forward and backward.

52. Lost Letter
The vowel not used is "A."

53. Fishing Fun
Three fishermen.

54. Lurking Letters
THE, THERE, HE, IN, REIN, HER, HERE, ERE, THEREIN, HEREIN.

55. What's for Supper?

H O T   D O G
4 10 3   22 10 14

56. Body Trivia
Eye, ear, lip, gum, jaw, arm, rib, hip, leg, toe.

57. Sneaky Sequence
The months of the year.

58. Sentence Structure

The sentence uses every letter in the alphabet.

59. Family Photo

The man in the riddle is the speaker's son.

60. Stick Shapes

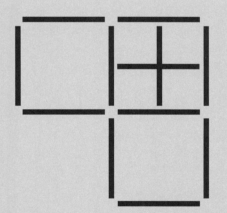

61. Car Caper

The four tires have all traveled the same distance of 45,000 miles.

62. Guess the Saying

Sick as a dog.

63. Calendar Calculus

All of them.

64. Proverb Palaver

An apple a day keeps the doctor away.
Every cloud has a silver lining.
Great minds think alike.
The early bird catches the worm.

65. Animal Antics

Roosters do not lay eggs.

66. Probability Pickle
3 socks.

67. Number Crunch
8 x 9 = 72.

68. Absolute Anagrams
QUEEN VICTORIA.

69. Look at the Line
T—each letter is the first letter of the numbers from one to 10.

70. Full House
Claire.

71. Picture Puzzle
Jack-in-the-box.

72. Fruit Swap
Chris has 7 apples and Phil has 5 apples.

73. Magic Trick
40.

74. Money Malarkey
The son answered 16 questions correctly out of 26. He got 10 wrong, so he owed his Dad 80 cents (10 x 8 cents) but his Dad owed him 80 cents (16 x 5 cents), so they were even.

75. Word Wonder

Each of the words becomes a new word when the letter "e" is placed after the first letter:
fear, below, beacon, leather, feasting, weariness, peacemaker.

76. Anagram Assortment

ATE, EAT, TEA.

77. Monkey Business

One, the zebra—all the other animals were going in the opposite direction.

78. Word Play

Move the first letter to the end of the word and it forms the same word backward.

79. What Can it Be?

Ton.

80. Flower Power

VIOLET, BUTTERCUP, LILY, TULIP.

81. Nimble Numbers

7 (seven) is the only number with two syllables.

82. Ant Antics

The ants were traveling in a circle.

83. What Do You See?

Safety in numbers.

84. Matchmaker

Japan—Flag B
Canada—Flag C
Greece—Flag A.

85. Raid the Fridge

BUTTER, MEAT, FRUIT.
(Use the first letter of each word.)

86. Bug Hunt

FLY.

87. Choppy Waters!

The boat rises with the waves
so no steps will be under water.

88. Smooth Sequence

T and V—they all rhyme.

89. Rodeo Riddle

His horse's name is "Friday."

90. Catch of the Day

There are only three people:
a grandfather, his son, and his
son's son.

91. Shady Puzzle

1. Opposite of summer
WINTER

2. Princesses usually wed a
PRINCE

3. Black and white striped African animals
ZEBRAS

4. Cows eat it and snakes lie in it
GRASS

5. An optical illusion in the desert
MIRAGE

6. Move to music
DANCE

The shaded squares spell out
WIZARD.

92. Journey Time

2 minutes—after one minute, the back of the train would be at the beginning of the tunnel. It would leave the end of the tunnel at two minutes.

93. Letter Jumble

SOLEMN, LEMONS, MELONS.

94. Wriggly Riddle

Snail.

95. Wordplay Array

REGAL, GLARE, LARGE.

96. Mind Melt
Your shadow.

97. Number Storm
$3 + 2 = 5 \times 10 = 50.$

98. Word Mix
PIRATE SHIP.

99. Flavor Frolics
CHOCOLATE, VANILLA, STRAWBERRY, MINT.

100. Guessing Game
Banana split.

101. Matchstick Movers
Result by moving three matchsticks.

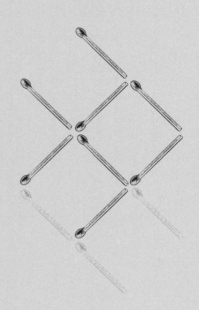

Crossword Puzzles

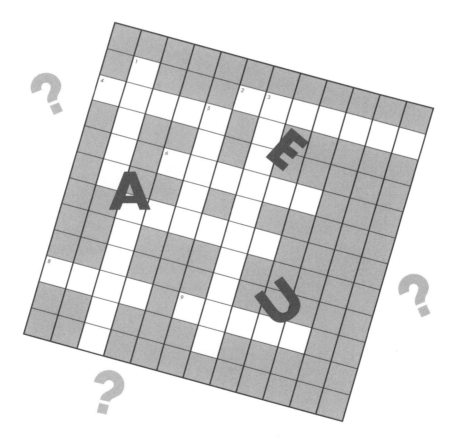

If you don't know all the answers, ask your parents if you can look them up on the Internet.

1. WILD ANIMALS

Across

1. The largest mammal in the ocean (5)
4. A predator with a sting in its tail (8)
6. A bird that often hunts at night (3)
8. An Asian ape with orange fur (9)
9. An egg-laying animal with a large shell (6)
10. A striped member of the horse family (5)

Down

2. A big cat with a shaggy mane (4)
3. A black and white flightless bird that swims (7)
5. A land and water reptile with huge jaws (9)
7. A fast African animal with hooves and horns (8)

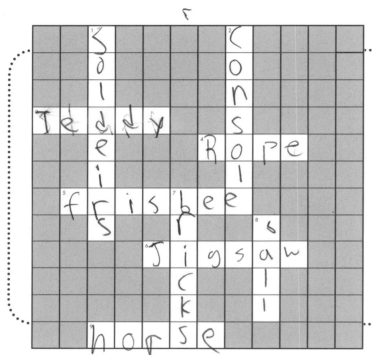

2. TOYS

Across

3. A stuffed cuddly toy (5)
4. A cord with handles for skipping (4)
5. A plastic disc for catching and throwing (7)
6. A picture puzzle with pieces that fit together (6)
9. A toy animal that rocks (5)

Down

1. Small fighting figures (8)
2. A machine that plays electronic games (7)
7. Building blocks (6)
8. A round toy that bounces (4)

3. WEDDINGS

Across

3. The man getting married (5)
4. The promises that a marrying couple make (4)
6. The bride and groom cut this after the wedding (4)
7. This is sometimes thrown at weddings (8)
8. A piece of jewelry worn by married people (4)
9. A book of pictures of the wedding (5)
10. What the bride wears (5)

Down

1. The holiday after the wedding (9)
2. A bunch of flowers carried by the bride (7)
5. The girl who walks behind the bride (10)

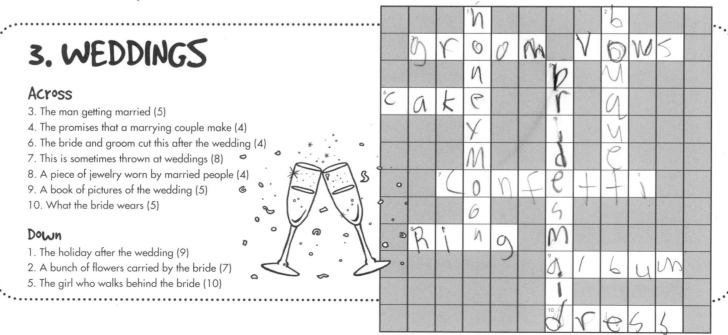

4. BIRTHDAYS

Across

3. An object blown up and tied with string (7)
4. A fun event on your birthday (5)
7. A note asking friends to your birthday event (10)
9. What you play at parties (5)
10. Something you do to music (5)

Down

1. An entertainer who does tricks (8)
2. Things you are given on your birthday (8)
5. You blow these out on your birthday (7)
6. Friends do this to the tune "Happy Birthday" (4)
8. Something you eat at your party (4)

(Crossword grid with handwritten answers: m, presents, balloon, party, magician, candles, invitation, singing, candle, games, cake, dance)

5. CHRISTMAS

Across

1. An evergreen plant to hang decorations on (4)
4. Presents that we post (7)
8. You pull these at the table (8)
10. Icy flakes that fall from the sky (4)

Down

2. Magical helpers who make toys (5)
3. Songs we sing at Christmas time (6)
5. A reindeer with a red nose (7)
6. A jolly man who climbs down chimneys (5)
7. Picture greetings sent at Christmas (5)

(Crossword grid with handwritten answers: tree, elves, rudolph, santa)

6. COUNTRIES

Across

1. You'll find haggis and kilts in this country (8)
3. The Great Wall was built across this country (5)
6. The Eiffel Tower and champagne are found here (6)
8. The country famous for Gurkha soldiers and Mount Everest (5)
9. Leprechauns are said to live here (7)

Down

1. A country known for flamenco and paella (5)
2. Kangaroos live here (9)
4. Don't cry for this South American country (9)
5. A country famous for curry and Bollywood (5)
7. The land of the Pyramids (5)

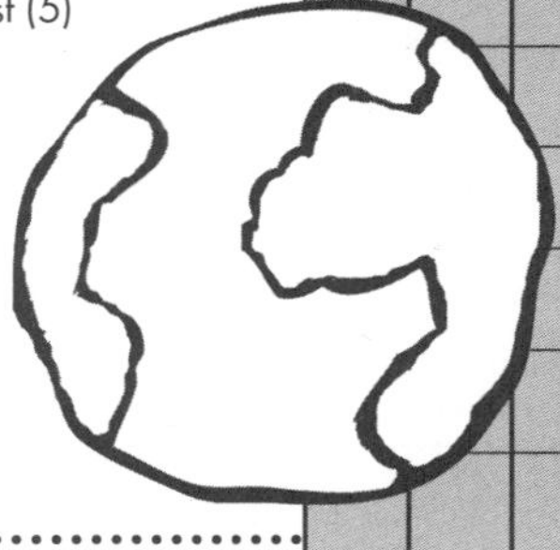

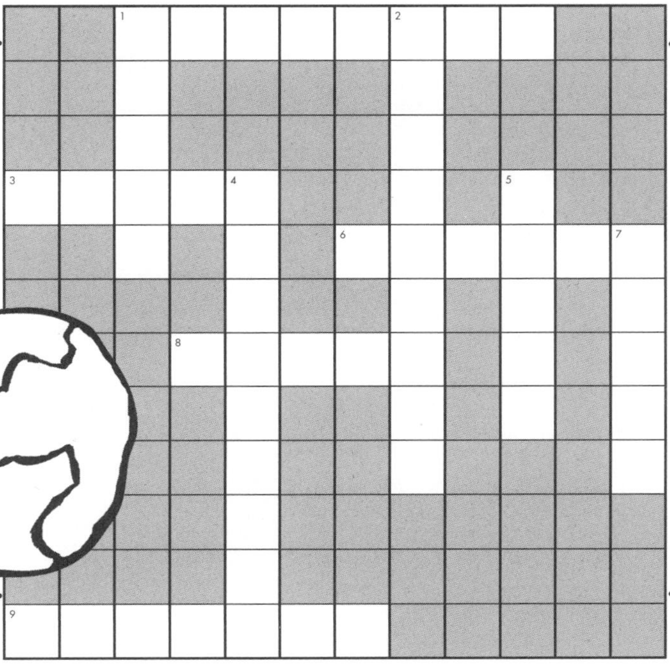

7. British Royals

Across

1. A king who was called "The Conqueror" (7)
4. A king who was said to be mad (6)
7. A queen who was married to Prince Albert (8)
8. A young king crowned at 9 years old and died aged 15 (6)
9. The first king of both England and Scotland (5)
10. The only British king to be beheaded (7)

Down

2. A queen known as "bloody" (4)
3. The king who had six wives (5)
5. The name of the longest reigning queen (9)
6. A king who was a hunchback (7)

8. UNDER THE SEA

Across

2. An animal with eight tentacles (7)
6. A craft that moves underwater (9)
7. A fish with famously wide jaws and sharp teeth (5)
8. A pretty object sometimes found in an oyster (5)
9. A scuttling creature with a shell and claws (4)
10. A mythical creature, half woman, half fish (7)

Down

1. A group of fish (5)
3. A plant that grows underwater (7)
4. A sunken boat (9)
5. An underwater coral habitat (4)
6. Swims upright, doesn't say "neigh" (8)

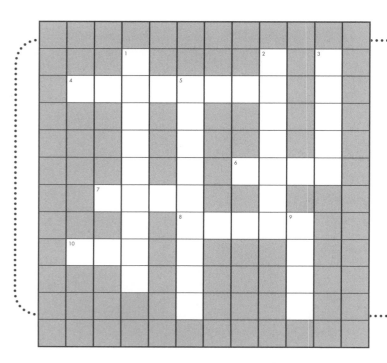

9. FLOWERS

Across

4. A blue flower found in woodlands in spring (8)
6. A waxy flower found on ponds (4)
7. A sweet-smelling flower with thorns (4)
8. The part of a plant that grows below the ground (5)
10. A yellow and black insect that visits flowers (3)

Down

1. A giant yellow flower with black seeds (9)
2. A person who sells flowers (7)
3. You can make a chain using this flower (5)
5. A wild, yellow cup-shaped flower (9)
9. The long green shaft that supports the flower (4)

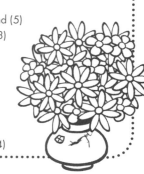

10. TREES

Across

2. The tiny flowers on tree branches (7)
5. Another word for the wood from trees (6)
7. A large area covered with trees (6)
8. A crunchy fruit grows on this tree (5)
9. This changes color in autumn (4)
10. The strong woody stem of the tree (5)

Down

1. A well-known weeping tree (6)
3. A fluffy-tailed animal that eats nuts (8)
4. A tree that does not lose its leaves (9)
6. A sweet syrup is made from this tree (5)

11. OCEAN COMMOTION

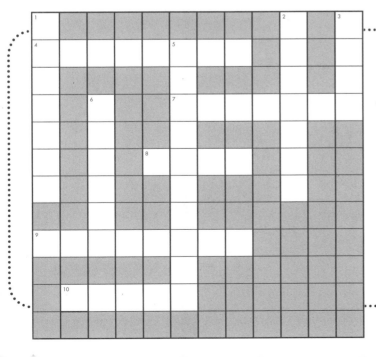

Across

2. A rogue of the high seas (6)
4. The rise and fall of sea levels (5)
6. A sailing vessel (4)
8. A gigantic wave (7)
10. Found in seawater but not in freshwater (4)

Down

1. An island shipwreck survivor (8)
3. Washed up tree branch (9)
5. An animal with tentacles that squirts ink (5)
7. A person who rides waves on a board (6)
9. Land surrounded by sea (6)

12. MYTHS AND LEGENDS

Across

4. A warrior with a weak heel (8)
7. A mythical horse with wings (7)
8. Another name for the abominable snowman (4)
9. A creature with a bull's head and a man's body (8)
10. A hooded man who led a group of merry men (5)

Down

1. King Arthur's castle (7)
2. Said to live in Loch Ness (7)
3. The Roman god of war and a planet (4)
5. Little person in Irish folklore (10)
6. Saint George killed this (6)

13. LANDMARKS

Across
1. Name of the bell in London's famous clock tower (3)
4. A New York statue holding a torch (7)
6. A metal tower in Paris (6)
8. Large tombs in Egypt (8)
10. A ring of ancient standing stones in England (10)

Down
2. A giant ferris wheel in London (3)
3. A fortress in Moscow with Red Square nearby (7)
5. The Queen's London palace (10)
7. A tower in Pisa (7)
9. The Sydney ____ House (5)

14. THE LETTER "S"

Across
1. You put this in food to sweeten it (5)
2. Another word for "yell" (5)
4. Moving in water (8)
6. A plank with wheels (10)
7. A basin in which you wash your hands (4)

Down
1. A type of extreme weather (5)
3. A slithering animal that hisses (5)
4. An activity performed on snowy slopes (6)
5. These keep your feet warm (5)
6. Hot liquid food (4)

15. THE LETTER "T"

Across
3. Used to see faraway planets (9)
4. Found on the end of a foot (3)
5. Something used for pouring tea (6)
7. A big, orange and black wildcat (5)
8. You use these devices for making things (5)

Down
1. An instructor at school who takes lessons (7)
2. A gadget used to talk to people far away (9)
5. A sport played at Wimbledon (6)
6. You use this to dry yourself (5)
7. A type of transport that runs on tracks (5)

16. IN THE KITCHEN

Across

1. A piece of cutlery with prongs (4)
2. A machine for cleaning dirty china (10)
6. A metal box for cooking food (4)
8. You eat your food off this (5)
9. This is used for cutting things (5)

Down

1. A box that keeps food chilled (6)
3. This sits on a hob to heat food (8)
4. You put this on before handling hot things (5)
5. This boils water (6)
7. Something you wear to protect your clothes (5)

17. CREEPY-CRAWLIES

Across

4. A black and yellow insect that stings (4)
5. It has eight legs and spins a web (6)
7. This insect is said to have 100 legs (9)
9. This insect does not breathe fire (9)

Down

1. It drinks blood and can carry disease (8)
2. A creepy-crawly with hard wing cases (6)
3. This larva changes inside a cocoon (11)
6. An insect that flies around lights in the dark (4)
8. This hides in damp places and has pincers (6)

18. HOBBIES

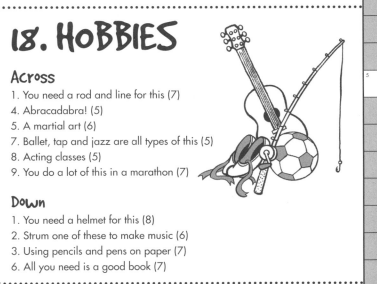

Across

1. You need a rod and line for this (7)
4. Abracadabra! (5)
5. A martial art (6)
7. Ballet, tap and jazz are all types of this (5)
8. Acting classes (5)
9. You do a lot of this in a marathon (7)

Down

1. You need a helmet for this (8)
2. Strum one of these to make music (6)
3. Using pencils and pens on paper (7)
6. All you need is a good book (7)

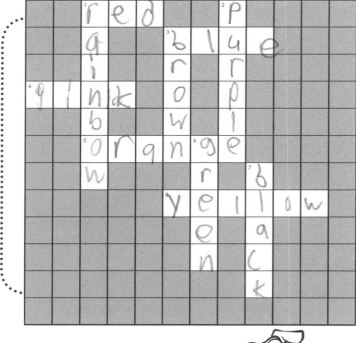

The completed crossword grid shows handwritten letters:
- red
- rainbow
- blue / brown
- purple
- pink
- orange / green
- yellow
- black

19. COLORS

Across
1. Your blood is this color (3)
3. The color of a sunny sky (4)
4. The color of cotton candy (4)
5. A fruit as well as a color (6)
8. The color of the sun (6)

Down
1. An arc of colors in the sky (7)
2. Blue and red mixed together (6)
3. The color of coffee and chocolate (5)
6. Grass is usually this color (5)
7. The color of a witch's cat (5)

20. PETS

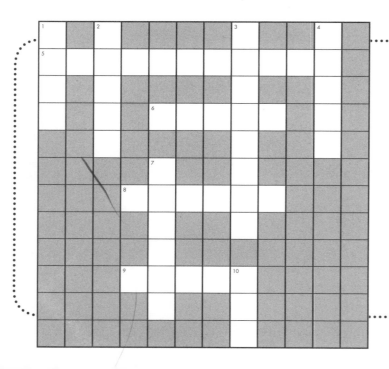

Across
4. An animal that purrs (3)
7. A slow animal with a shell (8)
8. A reptile with a flicking tongue (6)

Down
1. Blamed for once spreading the Black Death (3)
2. You can win these at the fairground (8)
3. It likes to run inside a wheel (7)
4. This is yellow and likes to tweet (6)
5. It lives in a cosy hutch (6)
6. A pet that squeaks (5)
9. Man's best friend (3)

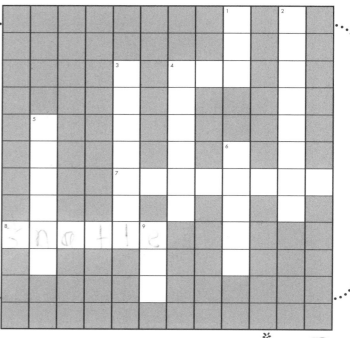

The grid shows handwritten letters: snaffle

21. MAGIC

Across
5. This word can transform things (11)
6. Another word for a charm (5)
8. A magical brew (6)
9. An old hag with magic powers (5)

Down
1. A special stick used to cast a spell (4)
2. This is used for sweeping or flying (5)
3. A large cooking pot to make foul brews in (8)
4. A tiny person with wings (5)
7. A small, naughty creature that lives in the woods (6)
10. A wizard wears this on his head (3)

22. DANCE

Across
2. An English folk dance with sticks, bells and handkerchiefs (6)
3. Eastern dancing using your tummy and hips (5)
4. A traditional Hawaiian dance (4)
5. Formal dances perfomed in pairs, such as the Waltz (8)
6. Hip hop dancing that began in public places (6)
9. Partners swing to rock and roll music (4)

Down
1. Country and western dancing in rows (4)
3. Dancers perform on tiptoe (6)
7. A fast, spinning folk dance (4)
8. Dancers wear shoes that click on the floor (3)

23. BOYS' NAMES

Across
2. This name rhymes with "manual" (6)
6. The female version is "Georgina" (6)
8. This person might be called "Bill" for short (7)
10. In the Bible, he survived the lion's den (6)

Down
1. One of Jesus's disciples (7)
3. The youngest son of Prince Charles (5)
4. Name that rhymes with "frames" (5)
5. "Alexandra" is the female version of this name (9)
7. An orphan who once asked.for more (6)
9. He fell down and broke his crown (4)

24. GIRLS' NAMES

Across
2. The male version of this name is "Oliver" (6)
6. An actress in "Fantastic Four" (7)
9. She wrote *Wuthering Heights* (5)
10. It rhymes with "snowy" (5)

Down
1. A large white flower (4)
3. "Bella" is a short form of this name (8)
4. She fell down a rabbit hole (5)
5. She wrote *Jane Eyre* (9)
7. She made friends with the BFG (6)
8. It rhymes with "Delia" (6)

25. SPORTS

Across
4. Players run with the ball and pass backward (5)
6. You do this in a boat with oars (6)
7. Fighting with swords (7)
9. Batting a shuttlecock over a net (9)
10. Track and field sports (9)

Down
1. Racing on a bicycle (7)
2. Shooting arrows at a target (7)
3. Players on horses knock a ball with sticks (4)
5. Dropping a ball through a high hoop (10)
8. Players call "Fore!" when they hit the ball (4)

26. AT THE SEASIDE

Across
3. An animal you can ride on the beach (6)
6. A model with turrets made from soft material (10)
8. A beach shed by the sea (3)
9. A fruity ice treat on a stick (5)
10. Soft between your toes and easy to dig (4)

Down
1. A container for holding water (6)
2. A stripy seat to sit on (9)
4. A person who makes sure swimmers are safe (9)
5. A large umbrella for hot weather (7)
7. Pretty objects that wash up on the shore (6)

27. IN THE FOREST

Across
1. The smallest branches of wood on a tree (5)
2. A shy animal with hooves and antlers (4)
5. An animal that sprays a bad-smelling liquid (5)
6. We breathe this gas and plants make it (6)
9. A type of forest found near the equator (8)

Down
1. They have trunks, branches and leaves (5)
3. A little mammal that squeaks (5)
4. A trail for people to walk along (8)
7. An animal that howls at night (4)
8. A furry red animal with a bushy tail and pointy nose (3)

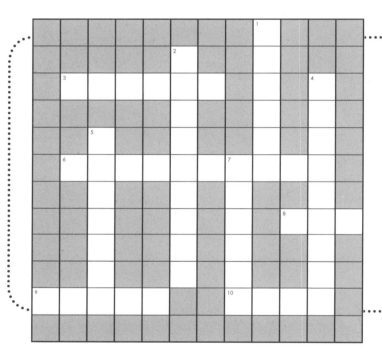

28. JOBS

Across
5. A person who cooks food in a restaurant (4)
7. Someone who finds the books for you to read (9)
8. This person helps sick animals (3)
9. You will learn from this person (7)
10. Florence Nightingale was one of these (5)

Down
1. Someone who puts out fires (11)
2. A news writer (10)
3. A person who fixes vehicles (8)
4. Criminals run away from this person (9)
6. Someone who constructs new houses (7)

29. At SCHOOL

Across
1. A collection of maps bound together (5)
3. Something to read (4)
7. Time to eat food in the middle of the day (9)
8. A note of how a pupil is doing at school (6)
9. Where you run around at recess (10)

Down
1. A gathering of pupils and teachers (8)
2. You learn how to use this in IT (8)
4. A wipe-clean screen (10)
5. Teacher takes this to see who is absent (8)
6. You use this to write and draw (6)

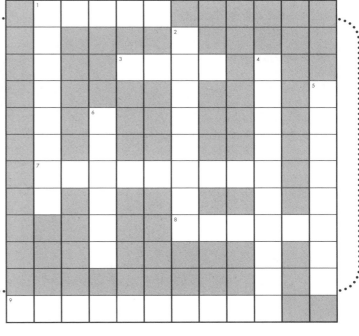

30. BABIES

Across
2. A song or verse for little children (5)
4. A baby drinks out of this (6)
7. A baby does this when it is not happy (6)

Down
1. A cup for babies and toddlers (5)
2. A toy babies shake to make a noise (6)
3. A baby's room (7)
5. Hanging toys above a baby's cradle (6)
6. Two babies born to the same mother on the same day (5)
7. A baby's bed (3)

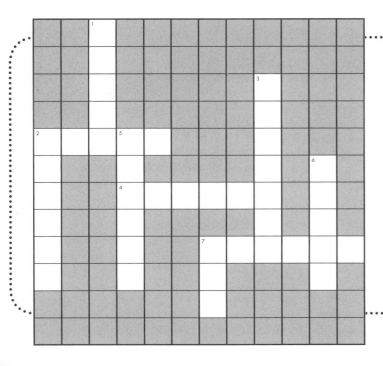

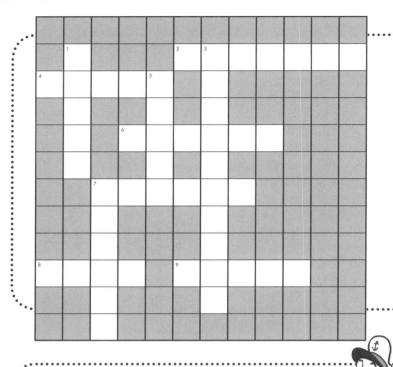

31. IN THE PARK

Across
2. A flat disc that you throw (7)
4. The green plant that grows on a lawn (5)
6. An outdoor meal on a blanket (6)
7. A plank with a seat at each end that tips up and down (6)
8. A watery home for fish and frogs (4)
9. Birds that go "quack!" (5)

Down
1. Metal poles for climbing on (5)
3. This spins you around again and again (10)
5. It has steps up, and a slippery chute down (5)
7. Seats dangling from chains that sway back and forth (6)

32. BOATS

Across
2. The sailor in charge (7)
5. These are used to row (4)
6. The steering board at the back of a ship (6)
8. A name for all the ropes aboard ship (7)
10. A room on board (5)

Down
1. The large canvas sheet that catches the wind (4)
3. A heavy weight thrown overboard to stop the boat (6)
4. The tall pole in the center of a sailing boat (4)
7. A powerboat needs this to move (6)
9. Something used to catch fish (3)

33. CINDERELLA

Across
1. A word to describe Cinderella's stepsisters (4)
3. A magical godmother (5)
6. She is unkind to Cinderella (10)
8. His name is Prince _____ (8)
9. A party at the palace (4)
10. The clock struck this time as Cinderella fled (8)

Down
2. Cinderella's slipper was made of this (5)
4. Cinderella got her name from sleeping beside this (9)
5. Cinderella's rags turn into this (4)
7. This was turned into Cinderella's coach (7)

34. ART

Across
3. A colored liquid for pens (3)
4. Color that can be brushed on to a surface (5)
5. A statue carved from hard material (9)
7. A picture of a person (8)
8. A painter's tool with bristles (5)

Down
1. A picture of the countryside (9)
2. An upright frame for a picture to rest on (5)
4. Making pots out of clay (7)
6. A stretched cloth for painting on (6)
7. Transfer a design on to paper or fabric (5)

35. EASTER

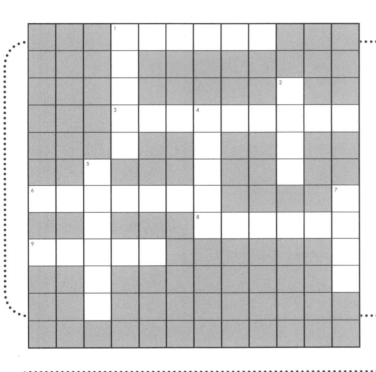

Across
1. The building where Christians worship (6)
3. Easter eggs are made of this (9)
6. Pretty plants that bloom (7)
8. The season when Easter is celebrated (6)
9. A bouncing Easter animal (5)

Down
1. A baby chicken (5)
2. A baby sheep (4)
4. The religious symbol of Easter (5)
5. You wear this on your head at Easter (6)
7. Birds lay these (4)

36. DESSERTS

Across
4. Whisked egg whites and sugar (8)
7. Flat batter tossed in a frying pan (7)
8. Layers of sponge, fruit and custard (6)
9. A very wobbly pudding (5)
10. A bitter yellow fruit (5)

Down
1. A biscuit base with a creamy top (10)
2. A mixture of flour and butter or oat mixture sprinkled on fruit (7)
3. A pastry base and lid with a filling (3)
5. A dairy product that is frozen (3,5)
6. Rhymes with "heart" (4)

37. FILMS

Across
3. A Native American princess (10)
4. A green ogre with a donkey sidekick (5)
5. A film about finding a fish with this name (4)
6. A superhero who lives in Gotham City (6)
7. This animal is King of the Pride Lands (4)
8. This fantasy film features James and a _____ peach (5)
10. Secret agent kids (3)

Down
1. Alice fell down a rabbit hole to find herself here (10)
2. The story of a lost Russian princess (9)
9. A cowboy called Woody and his friends feature in this story (3)

38. AT THE DINER

Across
1. It comes in sachets or bottles (5)
5. A seasoning that goes with salt (6)
6. Slices of bread with a filling (8)
9. A drink made with a bag and hot water (3)
10. A piece of furniture that you put your food on (5)

Down
2. A hot drink made from beans (6)
3. A tall, cold, frothy drink (9)
4. A list of dishes of the day (8)
7. You put this on your lap when eating (6)
8. A list of all the food and prices (4)

39. CLOTHES

Across
4. An undergarment with no sleeves (4)
6. It shows the price of an item (3)
8. This item only covers the upper leg (6)
10. Also known as a frock or gown (5)
11. They keep your feet warm and dry (5)

Down
1. A knitted top that buttons down the front (8)
2. A pair of pants with a bib attached (9)
3. Clothes for your legs (5)
5. These are for smart occasions (4)
7. A girl's garment that hangs from the waist (5)
9. These keep your head warm in the cold (4)

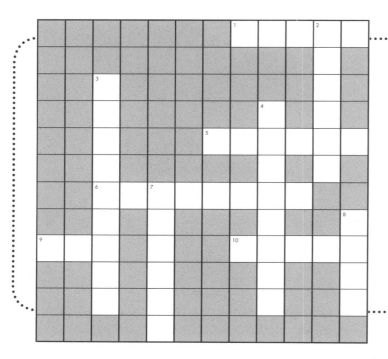

40. CLEANING

Across
4. A cleaner that sucks up dirt (6)
7. A type of duster on a stick (7)
8. A person who tidies up (7)
10. A wax that makes things shine (6)

Down
1. You use this to wash your hands (4)
2. Use a brush to sweep dirt into this (7)
3. Another word for germs (8)
5. A cloth used to clean plates (9)
6. A container with a handle for water (6)
9. A sponge or bundle of thick strings for washing floors (3)

41. IN YOUR BEDROOM

Across
1. A bedside light (4)
3. Things to play with (4)
7. Shelves for your reading material (8)
8. A basket for dirty washing (7)
9. A woven cloth to put on the floor (3)
10. You sleep in this (3)

Down
2. Pictures taken with a camera (11)
4. You hang your clothes in this (8)
5. A table on which to do your homework (4)
6. Something to sit on (5)

42. SPORTS DAY

Across
1. Four people take turns to complete a race (5)
3. A line you have to cross to win (6)
6. Competitors carry an egg in this (5)
7. A trophy given to a winner (3)
8. Winners are given these to wear (6)
9. A race when a person holds their friend's legs (11)

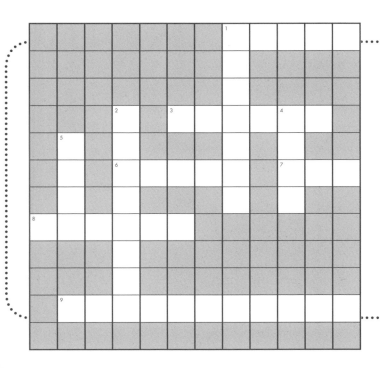

Down
1. Racing on foot (7)
2. You have to avoid things to win this race (8)
4. A large bag worn for a jumping race (4)
5. Tug of war needs a long one (4)

43. SOCCER

Across
1. Another name for a soccer arena (7)
2. A yellow or red one may be shown to players (4)
4. The person leading the team on the field (7)
7. The only player to play using his hands (10)
8. A record of the goals won by each team (5)

Down
1. A band of color on a shirt (5)
3. A sound that signals the start and end of a match (7)
5. The person who applies the rules during the game (7)
6. A mass of people watching the game (5)

44. BIRDS

Across
3. A talking bird (6)
7. A small caged bird that is a popular pet (10)
8. It has webbed feet and quacks (4)
9. It delivers new babies in fairy tales (5)

Down
1. It uses its beak to knock on trees (10)
2. This bird scoops up fish in its throat pouch (7)
3. Black and white bird with a large, colorful beak (6)
4. A bird with a red breast (5)
5. A tall, pink bird that stands on one leg (8)
6. This bird has a magnificent eyed tail (7)

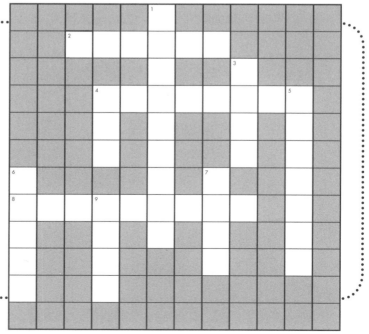

45. WEATHER

Across
2. White or gray, these hide the sun and may bring rain (6)
4. A weather report (8)
8. Streaks of electricity in the sky (9)

Down
1. A violent, whirling wind (9)
3. Water that falls from the sky (4)
4. Thick mist making it hard to see ahead (3)
5. The loud rumbling sound in storms (7)
6. Too much rain causes this (5)
7. Icy flakes falling from the sky (4)
9. Hard beads of ice (4)

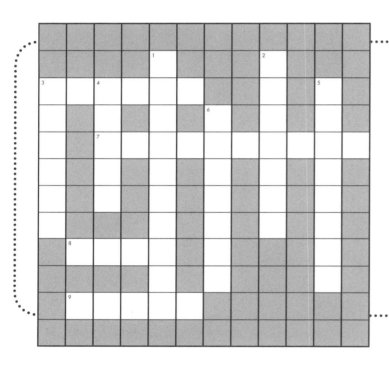

46. BABY ANIMALS

Across
1. A baby fox (3)
3. A baby horse (4)
5. A baby deer (4)
6. A baby duck (8)
9. A baby pig (6)

Down
1. A baby cow (4)
2. A baby goose (7)
4. A baby goat (3)
7. A baby cat (6)
8. A baby dog (5)

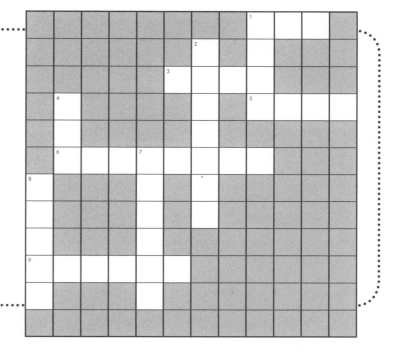

47. DRINKS

Across
3. A thin tube to suck liquid through (5)
5. A fizzy drink (4)
6. A popular brown fizzy drink (4)
8. A type of beer that children can drink (6)
9. A fruity drink made with milk or yogurt (8)

Down
1. The opposite of still water (9)
2. A drink made with lemons and sugar (8)
4. The liquid from squashed fruit (5)
7. A fruit flavor that is also a color (6)

48. MUSICALS

Across
2. A magical nanny called Mary _____ (7)
6. A clever girl in a Roald Dahl story (7)
7. A flying car that goes bang bang! (6)
8. The hills are alive with this sound (5)
10. A compass direction completes this name _____ Side Story (4)

Down
1. An orphan girl with curly red hair (5)
3. Follow the yellow brick road in this land (2)
4. Another word for "ghost" of the opera (7)
5. Beauty fell in love with this character (5)
9. Another word for "kitties" (4)

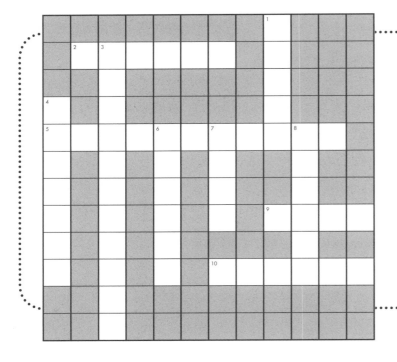

49. TELEVISION

Across

2. A program with more than one episode (6)
5. A factual programme (11)
9. A type of show and something you wash with (4)
10. A show that makes you laugh (6)

Down

1. A serious story (5)
3. A charge that powers the television (11)
4. Another word for "commercials" (7)
6. These are also called films (6)
7. An update on current events (4)
8. A hand control that changes TV channels (6)

50. HUMAN BODY

Across

2. These allow your arms to bend (6)
4. A skeleton is made of lots of these (5)
5. You'll find this in your mouth (6)
6. An organ that pumps blood around the body (5)
8. These hearing organs have drums! (4)

Down

1. The bend in your leg (4)
2. You need these to see (4)
3. Where food is digested (7)
6. These come in handy, one on each arm (5)
7. The fingers of your feet! (4)

51. CINEMA

Across

2. A list of the people who helped make a film (7)
5. The person who shows you to your seat (5)
6. A sweet or salty snack made from kernels (7)
7. A machine that shines the film on to a screen (9)
9. Commercials for upcoming films (8)
10. A strip of paper that lets you into the film show (6)

Down

1. The entrance hall of the cinema (5)
3. A word for the music and voices in the film (10)
4. A scary film (6)
8. You watch the film on this (6)

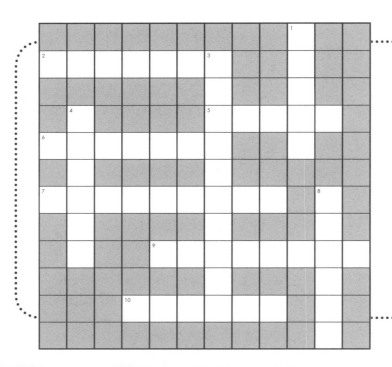

52. CATS

Across
4. A hopping insect that lives in cats' fur (4)
6. Long hairs that grow on a cat's face (8)
7. Something a cat does with its paws (7)
9. Cats like to drink this dairy product (4)
10. The happy noise that a cat makes (4)

Down
1. A long part at the end of a cat's body (4)
2. A small mammal that cats like to catch (5)
3. Sharp nails on a cat's paw (5)
5. She shares her broom with a black cat (5)
8. A band worn around a cat's neck (6)

53. SHOPPING

Across
2. Things you buy to wear (7)
6. At this store they sell bread and cakes (6)
7. A big store where you can do all your food shopping (11)
8. When you are tired, sit down here and have a coffee (4)
9. You wheel this around a supermarket (7)

Down
1. Prices go down when stores have one of these (4)
3. The main street of a town with lots of shops (10)
4. You buy everyday food items in this store (7)
5. Use your computer to shop this way (6)

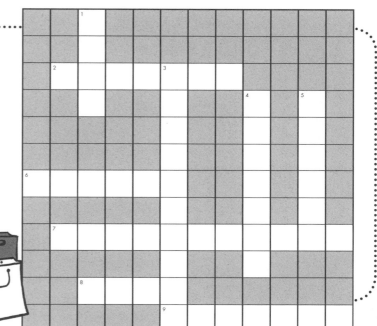

54. CHARACTERS

Across
3. A baby deer whose best friend is Thumper (5)
7. Beatrix Potter's hedgehog, Mrs ___ (11)
8. A cub prince in *The Lion King* (5)
10. A wild man raised by apes (6)

Down
1. One hundred and one spotty dogs (10)
2. The Little Mermaid's crab friend (9)
4. A little girl who was the size of a finger (10)
5. A giant ape called King ___ (4)
6. The owner of a chocolate factory, Willy___ (5)
9. Tinkerbell's friend, Peter ___ (3)

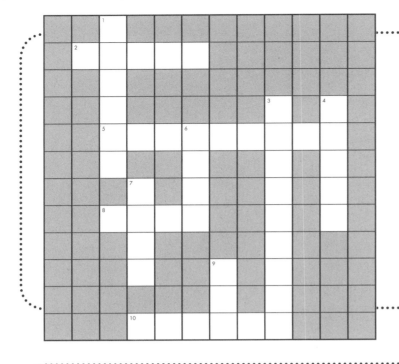

55. MUSIC

Across

2. Loud music, sometimes called heavy (5)
5. Singing without music (1,8)
8. Old country songs that are passed down (4)
10. A type of soulful music sung in some churches (6)

Down

1. A popular style of music from Jamaica (6)
3. Mozart and Beethoven wrote this kind of music (9)
4. This comes from Spanish-American countries (5)
6. Music for rebels (4)
7. Loud electric guitars and drums make this type of music (4)
9. Half-spoken songs with a strong beat (3)

56. THEATER

Across

3. The words of a play for the actors to read (6)
5. Moveable objects on stage to help set the scene (5)
8. The events of a play (4)
9. What actors do (3)
10. First performance, the first _____ (5)
11. The group of actors in a play (4)

Down

1. The platform where actors perform (5)
2. A booklet telling the audience about the play (9)
4. A heavy cloth that is opened and closed (7)
6. A circular light shone on an actor (9)
7. The break between the acts of the play (8)

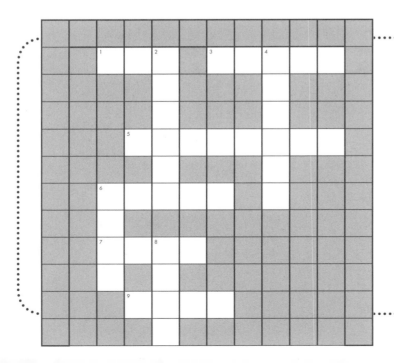

57. DOGS

Across

1. A doctor for animals (3)
3. A baby dog (5)
5. A black, golden or chocolate-colored gun dog (8)
6. A large fluffy dog used to pull sledges (5)
7. A daily outing (4)
9. The gruff sound a dog makes (4)

Down

2. Biscuits, bones and chews are these (6)
4. A breed that rhymes with "noodle" (6)
6. A dog cry (4)
8. A special rope that attaches to a dog collar (4)

58. HORSES

Across

4. Horses love this orange vegetable (6)
5. Dried grass that is very tasty (3)
7. A U-shaped band of iron that protects hooves (9)
9. The sound a horse makes (5)
10. A horse's shelter (6)

Down

1. An adult female horse (4)
2. Animal poo! (6)
3. A horse's fastest pace (6)
6. A rider in a horse race (6)
8. A leather seat for riders (6)

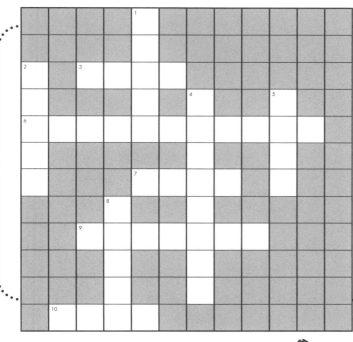

59. IN THE BACKYARD

Across

3. An animal similar to a frog (4)
6. A small pushcart with one wheel (11)
7. A wooden hut (4)
9. A place where bees live (7)
10. A twiggy home for birds (4)

Down

1. It has a spiral shell on its back (5)
2. A machine for cutting grass (5)
4. Giving plants a drink (8)
5. Wildlife lives in this water-filled hole (4)
8. Plants for flavoring food (5)

60. PIRATES

Across

4. What every pirate hopes to find (8)
5. A song about the sea (6)
6. Prisoners were forced to walk this (5)
7. This will show which direction you are sailing (7)
9. An object for looking into the distance (9)

Down

1. Some pirates wear this over one eye (5)
2. Metal balls are fired from this (6)
3. The Jolly Roger flag shows a skull and ___ (10)
6. A small handgun (6)
8. A call that sailors used when sighting land or a ship (4)

61. ON THE FARM

Across
4. A large pile of dried grass (8)
6. Another word for a rooster (8)
7. A large building where grain and equipment are stored (4)
9. The name for a group of cows (4)
10. A name for plants grown on a farm (5)

Down
1. The name for a group of sheep (5)
2. A famous old farmer in a nursery song (9)
3. A shelter for a pig (3)
5. A large vehicle that the farmer drives (7)
8. A fenced area for keeping animals (3)

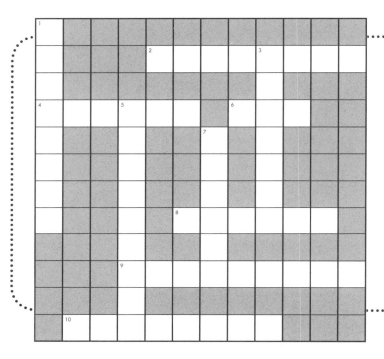

62. TRAINS

Across
2. A place where a train track cuts through a road (8)
4. The train moves along these (6)
6. The place where the driver sits (3)
8. This warns the driver when to stop and go (6)
9. A list of train schedules (9)
10. The passengers sit in this (8)

Down
1. A raised area where you wait for the train (8)
3. The train stops here to collect passengers (7)
5. The person who checks your ticket (9)
7. The locomotive that pulls the train (6)

63. SHAPES

Across
1. A shape that is also a precious gem (7)
3. A shape that is seen in the night sky (4)
7. This shape has three sides (8)
8. A squashed circle (4)
9. A six-sided shape (7)

Down
2. A shape with eight sides (7)
3. A box shape with four equal sides (6)
4. Another word for an oblong (9)
5. A ring shape (6)
6. A shape with five sides (8)

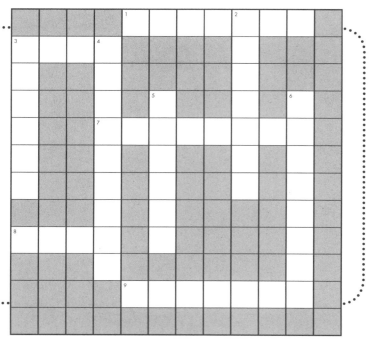

64. IN THE CAR

Across

3. These are found on the four wheels (5)
4. They clear rain from the windscreen (6)
5. You use this wheel to turn the car (8)
7. The pipe at the back of the car, from which gases escape (7)
9. Objects that let you see behind you (7)

Down

1. Wind these down to let air in (7)
2. A stick that changes the speed of the engine (4)
6. A signal showing which way the car will turn (9)
8. Apply these to stop (6)

65. BAKING

Across

1. A gadget used for beating (5)
3. They weigh ingredients (6)
9. A collection of recipes (8)
10. An ingredient that makes food sweet (5)

Down

2. Used to sift flour (5)
4. A small sponge with frosting (7)
5. A store selling bread and cakes (6)
6. You decorate cakes and buns with this (5)
7. A mixture is stirred in this (4)
8. An ingredient that makes bread rise (5)

66. CUISINE

Across

1. Seafood (4)
5. A flat, circular dough base with toppings (5)
8. A meat stew from Hungary (7)
9. Pasta layers with mince and sauce (7)
10. An Indian dish that can be very hot (5)

Down

2. Hot liquid food served in a bowl (4)
3. Cheesy tortilla chips with salsa (6)
4. Pasta strings served with Chinese food (7)
6. A dinner of meat, vegetables and gravy (5)
7. A meat patty in a bun (6)

67. AT THE AIRPORT

Across

4. The building where flights come in and out (8)
6. Passengers who have landed come through here (8)
7. Officials who check goods coming into the country (7)
8. Officials who check passengers for dangerous items (8)
9. A booklet that shows your identity (8)

Down

1. The head pilot (7)
2. Another word for a landing strip (6)
3. Passengers leaving the country go through here (10)
5. People's bags (7)
7. The staff who look after you on the airplane (4)

68. IN THE JUNGLE

Across

1. Another name for a snake's poison (5)
3. A group of people living together and sharing customs (5)
6. The natural home of a plant or animal (7)
8. A way that animals blend into the background (10)
10. A journey to explore the jungle (10)

Down

2. A species that no longer exists is this (7)
4. Lots of trees in a hot, wet climate (10)
5. The top, leafy layer of the forest (6)
7. The biggest rainforest in the world (6)
9. Apes swing from trees using these creepers (5)

69. CAMPING

Across

1. A warm bag to rest in at night (8,3)
3. Another name for a rucksack (8)
7. You look through these to see far away (10)
8. Strong cord used for tying things (4)
9. A wooden hut in the woods (5)

Down

2. The waterproof bottom layer of a tent that stops damp (11)
4. To put up a tent (5)
5. A long walk (4)
6. A wheeled room towed behind a car (7)

70. SPACE

Across

5. A person trained to go into space (9)
7. A creature from another world (5)
9. A flying space rock (6)
10. To circle around a planet (5)

Down

1. A circle or crescent shape in the night sky (4)
2. This keeps us grounded on Earth (7)
3. The blanket of gases around Earth (10)
4. Billions of stars (6)
6. The star that heats our planet (3)
8. It launches people into space (6)

71. MATH

Across

1. Do this to calculate the total of two or more numbers (3)
8. Circles and squares are these (6)
9. Another word for math (10)
10. You do this to find out how many (5)

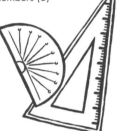

Down

2. Do this to split a number into equal parts (6)
3. To find the size of something (7)
4. To take away (8)
5. 1/2 and 1/4 are examples these (9)
6. To calculate the total of a number times another number (8)
7. Diagrams to show the relationships between two sets of numbers (6)

72. BOOKS

Across

3. Books about police and villains (5)
4. A series of events in a story (4)
6. Books about magic or imaginary worlds (7)
7. Books about love and relationships (7)
8. Someone who draws the pictures for a book (11)
9. A place that lends books (7)

Down

1. The person who wrote the book (6)
2. A short description on the back cover of a book (5)
3. A person in the book (9)
5. Another name for a "Whodunnit?" (7)

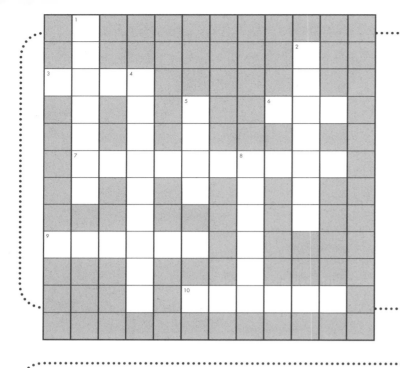

73. IN THE GYM

Across

3. The foods you eat regularly (4)
6. A flat cushion for the floor (3)
7. Something you bounce on (10)
9. A machine with oars and a sliding seat (6)
10. You can see your reflection in this (6)

Down

1. Heavy objects that you lift to build muscle (7)
2. A personal _____ helps people get fit (8)
4. A machine that you walk or run on (9)
5. Long cord that you skip with (4)
8. A safe box in which to keep your clothes (6)

74. HISTORICAL FIGURES

Across

2. A Victorian writer who wrote *Oliver Twist* (7)
5. This Jane wrote *Pride and Prejudice* (6)
7. Anne wrote a secret diary during the war (6)
9. Rosa ____ sat down for her rights (5)
10. Martin Luther Junior's last name (4)

Down

1. He composed at the age of 5 (6)
3. Britain's Prime Minister during World War II (9)
4. Emmeline fought for women's rights (9)
6. A famous scientist who was called Albert (8)
8. She experimented with radioactivity and won a Nobel Prize (5)

75. SCIENCE

Across

3. The study of living things (7)
5. A tall glass cylinder in which to test chemicals (4)
7. A gas flame comes from a Bunsen ___ (6)
9. A piece of iron that attracts other metals (6)
10. A thin tube that sucks up liquid (7)

Down

1. Facts that you gather from your observations (4)
2. An instrument for measuring temperature (11)
4. A room equipped for scientific experiments (10)
6. The study of substances and how they change (9)
8. The study of matter, energy and motion (7)

76. THE LETTER "R"

Across
2. Another name for a burglar (6)
5. An arc of colors in the sky (7)
6. Something you can only listen to (5)
8. A member of the Queen's family (5)

Down
1. A place to eat a nice meal (10)
2. A pretty strip of fabric to tie up hair (6)
3. A cowboy's home (5)
4. A pipe-like musical instrument (8)
6. You wear this piece of jewelry on your finger (4)
7. An animal that looks like a large mouse (3)

77. BOOK CHARACTERS

Across
2. Voldemort (4)
6. The color of a horse called Beauty (5)
8. The name of the doctor who made a monster (12)
9. The famous hobbit, ____ Baggins (5)
10. Romeo fell in love with her (6)

Down
1. Peter Pan fights this one-handed captain (4)
3. The wizard headmaster of Hogwarts (10)
4. A black and white character in *The Wind in the Willows* (6)
5. The lion in *The Lion, the Witch and the Wardrobe* (5)
7. He wins a visit to a chocolate factory (7)

78. CANDIES

Across
4. A chewy white candy bar made with honey, nuts and sometimes fruit (6)
5. Chew this but don't swallow it (3)
7. A sweet, fizzy powder (7)
8. Sugar animals with string tails (4)
9. A hard, sugary ball on a stick (8)
10. A sweet block made from milk and cocoa (9)

Down
1. Rhymes with "coffee" (6)
2. These spongy sweets are usually pink and white (12)
3. Rhymes with "sludge" (5)
6. A stripy, hard-boiled sweet from Britain (6)

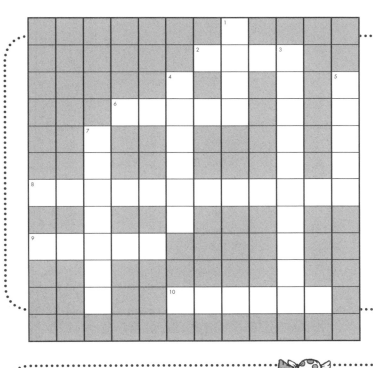

79. POST OFFICE

Across
1. You use this to post a letter (5)
6. A sealable wrapper to put a note in (8)
7. These measure the weight of mail (6)
9. Post delivered by airplane (7)

Down
1. You use this to tie around large items (6)
2. A man who delivers mail to your door (7)
3. Another word for "mail" (7)
4. A large, wrapped box (6)
5. The metal box that you put mail in (7)
8. An illustrated note sent on special occasions (4)

80. MONEY

Across
1. A building that keeps your money safe (4)
3. A plan of how you will spend your money (6)
6. Some money put away for the future (7)
7. Paying a small amount of a total price to reserve an item (7)
9. Money that you have borrowed and must pay back (4)
10. Coins left over from a payment (6)

Down
2. Another word for bills (5)
4. Money that you have given to charity (8)
5. Something you can use instead of cash (4)
8. A secret number that you use at a cash machine (3)

81. HOSPITAL

Across
4. To perform surgery (7)
8. A medical vehicle with flashing lights (9)
9. A medical practioner (6)
10. Someone who cares for sick people in hospital (5)

Down
1. An unexpected crisis (9)
2. Plaster put around a broken bone (4)
3. A doctor uses this to listen to your heartbeat (11)
5. An emergency first aid helper (9)
6. Patients are carried on this (9)
7. Someone who operates on sick people (7)

82. ARTS AND CRAFTS

Across

1. Making patchwork bedspreads (8)
5. Shaping timber with a sharp tool (11)
6. Something made from knotting and twisting fine thread (4)
7. Making cloth on a frame (7)
9. Arranging flowers (9)
10. A picture made from small tiles (6)

Down

2. Decorating with sugar (5)
3. Something pretty that people wear, made from metal and stones (7)
4. Folding paper to make objects (7)
8. A surface needed to paint a stained window (5)

83. THE LETTER "B"

Across

1. An explosive object (4)
3. You can cross over water or roads on this (6)
4. Your eyelids opening and closing quickly (8)
5. A yellow hair color (6)
7. A large, blazing heap of wood outdoors (7)
8. The skull protects this organ (5)

Down

2. Pandas eat this tall woody plant (6)
3. A cloth over your eyes so you can't see (9)
5. The opposite of "sister" (7)
6. A game where you mark off numbers on a card (5)

84. OLYMPICS

Across

1. These symbols appear on the Olympic flag (5)
4. You are given one of these for winning (5)
5. An event consisting of five sports (10)
6. Someone who competes in track and field events (7)
8. Skiing, bobsleigh and skating are part of this Olympics (6)
9. The national song of the winner's country (6)

Down

2. The country where the first Olympics began (6)
3. Competitors from the same country (4)
4. A long-distance running race (8)
7. This is carried to light the Olympic flame (5)

85. ON VACATION

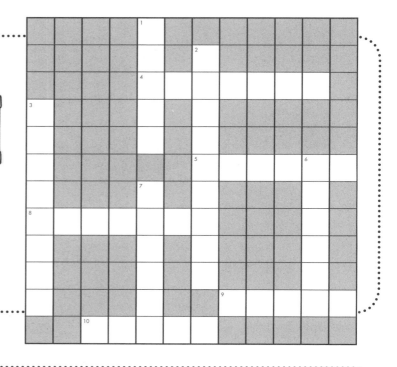

Across

4. Someone who travels on vacation (7)
5. A holiday on a ship (6)
8. Another word for "suitcases" (7)
9. A vehicle that travels on rails (5)
10. The sandy shore (5)

Down

1. A place to stay when away from home (5)
2. A lotion to protect skin from sunlight (9)
3. A vehicle you fly in (8)
6. A vacation to watch wild animals in their habitat (6)
7. You can take photographs with this (6)

86. AT THE DENTIST

Across

3. A dentist wears this over their mouth and nose (4)
4. A high-speed machine that removes tooth decay (5)
5. It packs a hole in a rotten tooth (7)
6. The soft tissue around your jaw (4)
7. Metal tracks that straighten your teeth (6)
9. A liquid you gargle with (9)

Down

1. A name for the four pointed teeth (6)
2. A deposit on teeth that can cause decay (6)
4. Another word for "false teeth" (7)
8. The part of a tooth that fixes into the jaw (4)

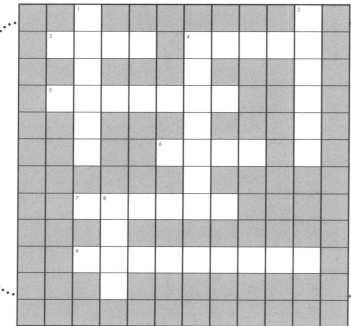

87. MUSIC INSTRUMENTS

Across

4. It rhymes with "yellow" (5)
7. A small drum with metal disks around the edge (10)
8. A large, angelic stringed instrument that is plucked (4)
9. A drum and also a kitchen item for making hot drinks (6)
10. It has a keyboard and pedals (5)

Down

1. The person who directs an orchestra (9)
2. Wooden bars of different lengths hit with a hammer (9)
3. A wooden tube with a double reed you blow through (4)
5. A thin pipe that is played by blowing air across a hole at one end (5)
6. It is also called a fiddle (6)

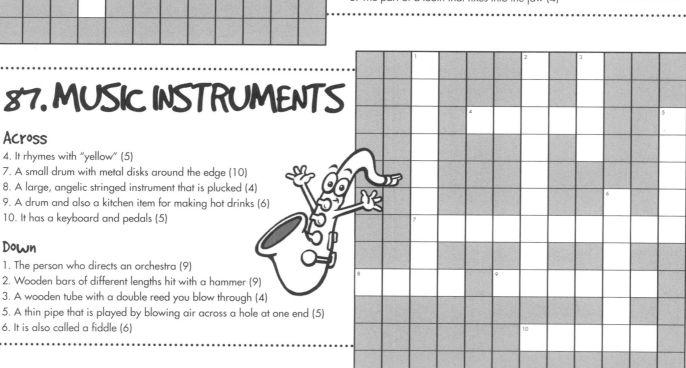

88. THE LETTER "M"

Across
1. An extinct elephant (7)
3. An orange jam spread on toast (9)
5. An old-fashioned gun (6)
7. The third month of the year (5)
8. A blind animal that burrows underground (4)

Down
2. A disease spread by mosquitoes (7)
3. Body tissue that gives us strength and movement (6)
4. Another word for "speechless" (4)
6. A man living in a religious community (4)
7. A traditional tale that can't be proved (4)

89. MAKE-UP

Across
2. A black pencil for the eyes (4)
5. Colored ink painted around the eyes, close to the lashes (8)
6. A product that thickens and colors the eyelashes (7)
8. Another word for "make-up" (9)
9. Powder colors for the eyelid (6)
10. Bristle tools used to apply make-up (7)

Down
1. A liquid that matches your skin color (10)
3. A powder to add color to the cheeks (7)
4. It makes the mouth shine (8)
7. A dust that stops your face shining (6)

90. EXTREME SPORTS

Across
4. A type of underwater diving using gas tanks (5)
6. Rolling downhill in a transparent, plastic orb (7)
7. Scaling high mountains (8)
8. To fly beneath a large, controllable canopy (9)
9. Stand up on a sailboard (8)

Down
1. You do this in "white water" (7)
2. To descend a steep drop quickly using ropes (6)
3. An elastic cord that ties around the ankles (6)
4. A leap out of an airplane (7)
5. You stand on this to slide down icy slopes (9)

91. MOVING HOUSE

Across
2. Money paid monthly to the landlord of a property (4)
4. Cardboard containers to store things in (5)
6. A board showing that a house is for sale (4)
8. The person who shows you around a new house (5)
9. These lock or unlock doors (4)
10. The place where you live and receive post (7)

Down
1. The _____ van moves your possessions (8)
3. The person who lives next door (10)
5. Moveable items, such as tables and chairs (9)
7. Putting things into crates (7)

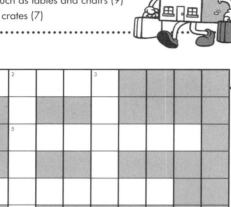

92. AT THE ZOO

Across
1. A large animal with a trunk (8)
5. A black and white flightless bird that swims (7)
6. It has thick skin and a horn on its head (10)
7. A cheeky creature that swings in trees using its long tail (6)
9. A large, hairy spider (9)
10. A long reptile that slithers (5)

Down
2. A large animal that wallows in swamps (12)
3. A big cat with black and orange stripes (5)
4. A slow-moving reptile with a shell (8)
8. A black and white bear (5)

93. AT THE CIRCUS

Across
3. Another word for "clapping" (8)
7. A safety mesh that catches you if you fall (3)
8. Another name for a gymnast (7)
9. A very high swing (7)
10. Someone who keeps many balls in the air (7)

Down
1. The circus tent is called the big ___ (3)
2. A funny performer who wears face paint (5)
4. This has a saddle and only one wheel (8)
5. The person who announces the circus acts (10)
6. Wooden poles that make a performer taller (6)

94. ROYALTY

Across

3. A soldier who protects the palace (5)
5. A chair that the monarch sits on (6)
6. A story, The ___ and the Pea (8)
8. A country ruled by the monarchy (7)
9. King Arthur's men of the Round Table (7)

Down

1. A female monarch (5)
2. The precious headdress worn by the monarch (5)
4. A ceremony to officially crown a new monarch (10)
6. The son of a monarch (6)
7. The ditch filled with water surrounding a castle (4)

95. THE LETTER "P"

Across

1. A picture taken by a camera (10)
3. A person who fixes water leaks (7)
4. A written verse (4)
6. Clothes you wear in bed (7)
7. The opposite of "starboard" (4)
8. Small stones on the seashore (7)

Down

1. A prickly tropical fruit (9)
2. An animal that hunts prey (8)
4. An uncomfortable feeling (4)
5. An artist who uses a brush (7)

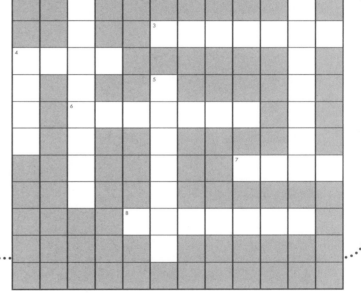

96. FRUIT

Across

2. A soft, red fruit with a stone inside (6)
5. A curved, yellow fruit that you peel (6)
7. Rhymes with "thumb" (4)
9. A soft, red fruit with pips on the outside (10)
10. A juicy yellow-fleshed fruit with a fuzzy skin (5)

Down

1. Rhymes with "bear" (4)
3. A fruit that also means a rude noise (9)
4. A green, sour fruit (4)
6. Eve gave one of these to Adam (5)
8. These grow in a bunch (6)

97. TRANSPORT

Across
2. An armored vehicle used by the army (4)
3. This can be a single or double-decker vehicle (3)
4. A four-wheeled vehicle suitable for a family (3)
7. A two-wheeled, engine-powered cycle (9)
9. A small delivery truck (3)

Down
1. The name of the subway in London (11)
3. It has two wheels, pedals and handlebars (7)
5. An electric carriage that travels on road rails (4)
6. A car that carries passengers for a fee (4)
8. A craft that travels on water (4)

98. EMOTIONS

Across
1. Angry and annoyed (5)
4. Baffled and bewildered (8)
8. Merry and cheerful (5)
9. Eager and enthusiastic (7)
10. Calm and chilled (7)

Down
2. Glum and gloomy (3)
3. Everything feels just right (7)
5. Scared and anxious (10)
6. Bashful and blushing (3)
7. In need of sleep (5)

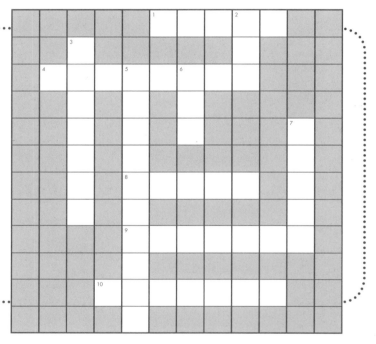

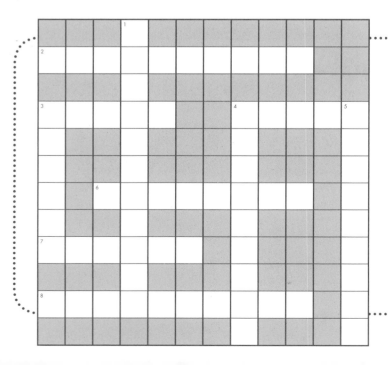

99. THE LETTER "W"

Across
2. Material that stops rain from getting in (10)
3. A ballroom dance (5)
4. A woman whose husband has died (5)
6. Age lines in the skin (8)
7. A man who has magical powers (6)
8. A circular object turned by a stream (10)

Down
1. It shows which way the wind is blowing (11)
3. Glass in a wall that lets you see out (6)
4. Sheets pasted around a room (9)
5. A river cascading over a cliff (9)

100. FURNITURE

Across

5. A cabinet where you keep novels (8)
6. Somewhere to sleep (3)
7. Ledges of wood on which to put objects (7)
9. A chair that moves gently backward and forward (7)
10. Sliding compartments to put things in (7)

Down

1. Two places to sleep, one above the other (4)
2. A flat surface on legs where you eat (5)
3. A decorative hanging light with branches (10)
4. A place to display and store plates and cups (7)
8. Another name for a couch or settee (4)

101. DANCING

Across

2. A long snake of people dancing around the room (5)
3. Some schools have this big party to celebrate graduation (4)
4. Music blasts from these (8)
5. The day before the weekend (6)
7. These flash on and off to make a cool atmosphere (6)
8. An energetic street dance, with spins on the floor (10)

Down

1. Moving to the music (7)
2. They might have one of these to find the best dancer! (11)
6. The surface on which you dance (5)

ANSWERS

1. WILD ANIMALS

W H A L E P
I E
S C O R P I O N N
R N G
O W L A U
C A I
O R A N G U T A N
D E
I T U R T L E
L O
Z E B R A P
E

2. TOYS

S C
O O
L N
T E D D Y S
I R O P E
E L
F R I S B E E
S R B
J I G S A W
C L
K L
H O R S E

3. WEDDINGS

H B
G R O O M V O W S
N B U
C A K E R Q
Y I U
M D E
C O N F E T T I
O S
R I N G M
A L B U M
I
D R E S S

4. BIRTHDAYS

M
P B A L L O O N
P A R T Y G
E I
S C
E S I C
I N V I T A T I O N
T N N D
S G C L
G A M E S
K S
D A N C E

5. CHRISTMAS

T R E E
L
V C
P A R C E L S T A
U S U R
D A R O
O N K L
C R A C K E R S
P A Y
H R
D
S N O W

6. COUNTRIES

SCOTLAND
SPAIN
AUSTRALIA (partial: A,U,S,T,R,A... down)
CHINA
ARGENTINA
FRANCE
NEPAL
IRELAND
EGYPT
INDIA

7. British Royals

WILLIAM
MARY
HENRY
GEORGE
GEORGE
RICHARD
VICTORIA
ELIZABETH
EDWARD
JAMES
CHARLES

8. UNDER THE SEA

SHOALES
OCTOPUS
SUBMARINE
SHARK
PEARL
CRAB
MERMAID
SEAWEED
SHIPWRECK
REEF

9. FLOWERS

SUNFLOWER
FORGETMENOT
DAISY
BLUEBELL
BUTTERCUP
LILY
ROSE
ROOTS
STEM
BEE

10. TREES

WILLOW
BLOSSOM
SEQUOIA
EVERGREEN
TIMBER
MAPLE
FOREST
APPLE
LEAF
TRUNK

11. OCEAN COMMOTION

CAST
PIRATE
DRIFTWOOD
SHIP
STINGRAY
TSUNAMI
TIDES
SEASQUID
ISLAND
SALT

12. MYTHS AND LEGENDS

CAMELOT
ACHILLES
MEDUSA
DRAGON
MERMAID
PEGASUS
YETI
MINOTAUR
ROBIN

13. LANDMARKS

BEN
BYE
KREMLIN
LIBERTY
EIFFEL
BUCKINGHAM
PYRAMIDS
STONEHENGE
OPERA

14. THE LETTER "S"

SUGAR · SHOUT · STORE · SNAKE · SWIMMING · SKIING · SKATEBOARD · SOUP · SOCKS · SACK · SINK

15. THE LETTER "T"

TELESCOPE · TEACH · TOE · TEAPOT · TIGER · TRAIN · TENNIS · TOOLS · TELEPHONE · TOWEL

16. IN THE KITCHEN

FORK · FRIDGE · DISHWASHER · WASHER · GLOVE · OVEN · APRON · PLATE · KNIFE · KETTLE · SAUCEPAN

17. CREEPY-CRAWLIES

MOSQUITO · BEETLE · CATERPILLAR · WASP · SPIDER · MOTH · CENTIPEDE · DRAGONFLY · EARWIG

18. HOBBIES

FISHING · GUITAR · DRAWING · MAGIC · KARATE · BASEBALL · DANCE · READING · DRAMA · RUNNING

19. COLORS

RED · BLUE · PINK · ORANGE · YELLOW · RAINBOW · BROWN · PURPLE · GREEN · BLACK

20. PETS

RAT · GOLDFISH · HAMSTER · CAT · CANARY · RABBIT · TORTOISE · MOUSE · LIZARD · DOG

21. MAGIC

WAND · BROOM · CAULDRON · FAIRY · ABRACADABRA · SPELL · GOBLIN · POTION · WITCH · HAT

22. DANCE

- MORRIS
- L / N / E / A / L / E / L (vertical letters)
- BELLY
- HULA
- BALLROOM
- STREET
- T / A / P
- JIVE

23. BOYS' NAMES

- M
- SAMUEL
- H / J
- A / A / A
- T / L / R / M
- GEORGE
- O / X / Y / S
- WILLIAM
- N / I / D
- J / V / E
- DANIEL
- C / R / R
- K

24. GIRLS' NAMES

- L
- OLIVIA
- S / L / A / C
- A / Y / L / H
- B / I / A
- JESSICA
- R
- L / O / EMILY
- L / P / E / O
- A / H / L / T
- I / I / T
- CHLOE / A / E

25. SPORTS

- C
- A / P / Y
- RUGBY / O / C
- C / A / L / L
- H / S / ROWING
- E / K / N
- R / FENCING
- Y / T / G
- BADMINTON
- A / L
- L / F
- ATHLETICS

26. AT THE SEASIDE

- B
- D / U
- DONKEY / C / L
- C / K / I
- P / K / E / F
- SANDCASTLE
- R / H / H / G
- A / A / E / HUT
- S / I / L / A
- O / R / L / R
- LOLLY / SAND

27. IN THE FOREST

- TWIGS
- DEER / E / M
- E / O
- FOX / SKUNK
- O / S
- OXYGEN
- T
- P / W
- A / F / O
- TROPICAL
- H / X / F

28. JOBS

- F / J / M
- I / O / E
- R / U / P / C
- CHEF / R / O / H / B
- F / N / L / A / U
- LIBRARIAN / I / I
- G / L / C / L
- H / I / C / D
- VET / S / M / E
- E / TEACHER
- NURSE / N

29. AT SCHOOL

- ATLAS
- S / C
- S / BOOK / W
- E / M / H / R
- M / P / P / I / E
- B / E / U / T / G
- LUNCHTIME / I
- Y / C / E / B / S
- I / REPORT
- L / A / E
- PLAYGROUND

30. BABIES

Across/Down words filled in grid:
TIPPY
NURSE
RHYME
BOTTLE
TWINS
CRYING
RATTLE
COT

31. IN THE PARK

FRISBEE
GRASS
FRAME
PICNIC
SEESAW
POND
DUCKS
SWING
SLIDE
ROUNDABOUT

32. BOATS

SAIL
CAPTAIN
ANCHOR
MAST
OARS
RUDDER
ENGINE
RIGGING
CABIN

33. CINDERELLA

UGLY
SLIPPER
FAIRY
STEPMOTHER
GLASS
FIREPLACE
PUMPKIN
CHARMING
BALL
MIDNIGHT

34. ART

LANDSCAPE
EASEL
INK
PAINT
SCULPTURE
POTTERY
PORTRAIT
PRINT
CANVAS
BRUSH

35. EASTER

CHURCH
CHICK
LAMB
CHOCOLATE
CROSS
BONNET
FLOWERS
SPRING
EGGS
BUNNY

36. DESSERTS

CHEESE
CRUMBLE
PIE
MERINGUE
ICECREAM
TART
PANCAKE
TRIFLE
JELLO
LEMON

37. FILMS

WONDERLAND
ANTASTA
POCAHONTAS
SHREK
NEMO
BATMAN
LION
GIANT
SPY

38. AT THE DINER

Across/Down filled letters:
- SAUCE
- COFFEE (down)
- MILK (down)
- SPEPPER / PEPPER
- SANDWICH
- TEA / TABLE
- TAKEN (down)
- NAPKIN (down)
- MENU (down)
- CHILIS (down)

39. CLOTHES

- CARDIGAN
- DUNGAREE (down)
- PANT (down)
- VEST
- TIE
- SHORTS
- TAG
- SKIRT (down)
- SHEET (down)
- DRESS
- SHOES

40. CLEANING

- SOAP (down)
- DUSTPAN (down)
- BACTERIA (down)
- DISINFECT (down)
- BUCKET (down)
- VACUUM
- FEATHER
- CLEANER
- MOP (down)
- POLISH

41. IN YOUR BEDROOM

- LAMP
- PHOTOGRAPHS (down)
- TOYS
- WARDROBE (down)
- DESK (down)
- CHAIR (down)
- BOOKCASE
- LAUNDRY
- RUG
- BED

42. SPORTS DAY

- RELAY
- RUN (down)
- OF (down)
- FINISH
- SACK (down)
- ROPE (down)
- BST (down)
- SPOON
- CUP
- MEDALS
- WHEELBARROW

43. SOCCER

- STADIUM
- STILE (down)
- WHISTLE (down)
- CARD
- CAPTAIN
- REFEREE (down)
- CREW (down)
- GOAL KEEPER
- SCORE

44. BIRDS

- WOOD (down)
- PELICAN (down)
- FLAMINGO (down)
- PARROT
- PUFFIN (down)
- PEACOCK (down)
- BUDGERIGAR
- DUCK
- STORK

45. WEATHER

- HURRICANE (down)
- CLOUDS
- RAIN (down)
- FORECAST
- FOG
- SNOW (down)
- THUNDER (down)
- FLOOD (down)
- LIGHTNING

46. BABY ANIMALS

```
                  C U B
            G     A
          F O A L
    K       S   F A W N
    D U C K L I N G
P       I       N
U       T
P I G L E T     T
Y       N
```

47. DRINKS

```
            S                 L
            P                 E
S T R A W   J       M
        R   U     S O D A
        K   I
        L   C O L A   D
      G I N G E R   A   E
        N           N
        G           G
S M O O T H I E     G
```

48. MUSICALS

```
              A
    P O P P I N S     B
    Z     H   N       E
      M A T I L D A
      N     E         S
  C H I T T Y         T
      O
        M U S I C
          W E S T S
```

49. TELEVISION

```
              D
  S E R I E S R
  L           A
A E           M
D O C U M E N T A R Y
V   T   O   E   E
E   R   V   W   M
R   I   I   S   S O A P
T   C   E       T
S   I   S   C O M E D Y
    I
    Y
```

50. HUMAN BODY

```
                  K
E L B O W S   B O N E S
E     S       E
E     T O N G U E
S     M
    H E A R T
    A   C   O
    N   H   E A R S
    D       S
    S
```

51. CINEMA

```
            F
C R E D I T S O
        O   Y
    H   U S H E R
P O P C O R N   R
    R   D
    P R O J E C T O R S
    R   T R A I L E R S
    T I C K E T   E
                  E
                  N
```

52. CATS

```
  T           M
  A   C       O
  I   L       U
F L E A   W   S
    W H I S K E R S
    S     T
      S C R A T C H
      H       O
              L
          M I L K
              A
          P U R R
```

53. SHOPPING

```
      S
      A
    C L O T H E S
      E     I     G   O
            G     R   N
            H     O   L
B A K E R S       C   I
            T     E   N
      S U P E R M A R K E T
            E     Y
      C A F E
      T R O L L E Y
```

54. CHARACTERS

Across/filled answers:
- BAMBI
- TIGGYWINKLE
- SIMBA
- TARZAN

Down letters visible: DALMATIAN, SEBASTIAN, KOANAN, WASTSONAL, THUMBELINA, PAN

55. MUSIC

- METAL
- ACAPPELLA
- FOLK
- GOSPEL

Down: REGGAE, ROCK, CLASSICAL, LATIN, RAP, RICA, etc.

56. THEATER

- SCRIPT
- PROPS
- PLOT
- ACT
- NIGHT
- CAST

Down: PROGRAM, SPOTLIGHT, CURTAIN, INTERVAL, STAGE

57. DOGS

- VET
- PUPPY
- LABRADOR
- HUSKY
- WALK
- BARK

Down: TREAT, POODLE, HOWL, WALK

58. HORSES

- CARROT
- HAY
- HORSESHOE
- NEIGH
- STABLE

Down: MANE, MARE, GALLOP, MANURE, JOCKEY, SADDLE

59. IN THE BACKYARD

- TOAD
- WHEELBARROW
- SHED
- BEEHIVE
- NEST

Down: SNAIL, MOWER, WATERING, POND, HERB

60. PIRATES

- TREASURE
- SHANTY
- PLANK
- COMPASS
- TELESCOPE

Down: PATCH, CANNON, CROSSBONES, PISTOL, ASHOY

61. ON THE FARM

- HAYSTACK
- COCKEREL
- BARN
- HERD
- CROPS

Down: FLOCK, MEADOW, STY, SACK, TRACTOR, PLOUGH

62. TRAINS

PLATFORM, CROSSING, STATION, TRACKS, CAB, CONDUCTION, ENGINE, TICKET(?), SIGNAL, TIMETABLE, CARRIAGE

63. SHAPES

DIAMOND, STAR, SQUARE, RECTANGLE, CRESCENT(?), OCTAGON, TRIANGLE, PENTAGON, OVAL, HEXAGON

64. IN THE CAR

WINDOW, GAS, TIRES, WIPERS, WINDSCREEN(?), STEERING, BRAKE, EXHAUST, MIRRORS

65. BAKING

WHISK, MIXER(?), SCALES, CUPCAKE, SIEVE, BAKERY, COOKBOOK, YEAST, BOWL, SUGAR

66. CUISINE

FISH, SOUP, NACHOS(?), PIZZA, ROAST, BURRITO(?), GOULASH, NOODLES, LASAGNE, CURRY

67. AT THE AIRPORT

CAPTAIN, RUNWAY, DEPARTURE, TERMINAL, LUGGAGE, ARRIVALS, CUSTOMS, CREW, SECURITY, PASSPORT

68. IN THE JUNGLE

VENOM, EXTINCTIONS, TRIBE, CANOPY, HABITAT, ATM(?), CAMOUFLAGE, AMAZON, VINES, EXPEDITION

69. CAMPING

SLEEPING BAG, GROUND SHEET, BACKPACK, FIT(?), HIT(?), CD(?), BINOCULARS, ROPE, CABIN

70. SPACE

- MOON
- GALAXY
- GO
- ASTRONAUT
- ATMOSPHERE
- ALIEN
- METEOR
- ROCKET
- ORBIT

71. MATH

- ADD
- DIVIDE
- MEASURE
- SUBTRACT
- MULTIPLY
- GRAPH
- FRACTION
- SHAPES
- ARITHMETIC
- COUNT

72. BOOKS

- AUTHOR
- CRIME
- PLOT
- BUBURB
- FANTASY
- ROMANCE
- ILLUSTRATOR
- LIBRARY
- MYSTERY
- CHARACTER

73. IN THE GYM

- WEIGHTS
- DIET
- TREADMILL
- MAT
- TRAMPOLINE
- ROWING
- MIRROR
- LOCKER
- ROPE

74. HISTORICAL FIGURES

- MOZART
- DICKENS
- PANKHURST
- AUSTEN
- EINSTEIN
- FRANK
- CHURCHILL
- PARKS
- KING

75. SCIENCE

- BIOLOGY
- THERMOMETER
- TUBE
- CHEMISTRY
- BURNER
- PHYSICS
- MAGNET
- PIPETTE
- DATA
- LAB
- LABORATORY

76. THE LETTER "R"

- RESTAURANT
- ROBBER
- RANCH
- RIBBON
- RAINBOW
- RADIO
- ROYAL
- RING

77. BOOK CHARACTERS

- HOLMES
- LORD
- DUMBLEDORE
- DRACULA
- BLACK
- FRANKENSTEIN
- BILBO
- JULIET

78. CANDIES

Across/down answers filled in grid:
NOUGAT, GUM, SHERBET, MICE, LOLLIPOP, CHOCOLATE
(T, M, F, N, O, U, G, A, T, G, U, M, F, F, R, D, F, F, S, G, H, F, E, S, H, E, R, B, E, T, U, E, M, M, I, C, E, M, A, B, L, L, O, L, L, I, P, O, P, U, L, G, L, C, H, O, C, O, L, A, T, E, W, S)

79. POST OFFICE

STAMP, ENVELOPE, SCALES, AIRMAIL
(S T A M P, P, O, S, T, L, P, R, I, N, G, T, E, A, M, A, T, T, P, C, E N V E L O P E, R, S, L, S C A L E S, T, A, B, A I R M A I L, O, D, X)

80. MONEY

BANK, BUDGET, SAVINGS, DEPOSIT, LOAN, CHANGE
(B A N K, O, T, B U D G E T, C, E, O, A, S A V I N G S, R, A, D E P O S I T, I, I, L O A N, O, C H A N G E)

81. HOSPITAL

OPERATE, AMBULANCE, DOCTOR, NURSE
(E, C, M, S, O P E R A T E, T, A, S, R, S, E, A, T, G, T, T, R A, S, E, R, H, A M B U L A N C E, O, E, R, C, T, S, D, G, Y, C, C, I, E, H, O, D O C T O R, E, P, N, N U R S E)

82. ARTS AND CRAFTS

QUILTING, WOODCARVING, LACE, WEAVING, FLORISTRY, MOSAIC
(Q U I L T I N G, J, C, E, O, I, W O O D C A R V I N G, E, I, G, L A C E, G, R, W E A V I N G, Y, G, M, F L O R I S T R Y, A, S, M O S A I C)

83. THE LETTER "B"

BOMB, BRIDGE, BLINKING, BLONDE, BONFIRE, BRAIN, BROTHER, BLEND, BINGO
(B O M B, B, A, B R I D G E, M, L, B L I N K I N G, O, N, B L O N D E, B, B R, F, B O N F I R E, O, L, N, T, D, G, H, O, E, B R A I N)

84. OLYMPICS

RINGS, MEDAL, PENTATHLON, ATHLETE, WINTER, ANTHEM
(R I N G S, T, R, E, E, M E D A L, E, A, M, C, R, P E N T A T H L O N, T, A T H L E T E, O, O, W I N T E R, C, A N T H E M)

85. ON VACATION

HOTEL, TOURIST, CRUISE, LUGGAGE, TRAIN, BEACH, AIRPLANE, SEAFARER
(H, O, S, T O U R I S T, A, E, N, I, L, S, R, C R U I S E, P, C, R, A, L U G G A G E, F, A, A, M, E, A, N, E, N, R, E, R, T R A I N, B E A C H)

86. AT THE DENTIST

Across/Down answers visible:
- CONFINE (C-O-N-F-I-N-E)
- MASK
- DRILL
- PLAQUE
- FILLING
- GUMS
- BRACES
- MOUTH

Letters: C, P, MASK, DRILL, PLAQUE, CONFINE, FILLING, GUMSER, BRACES, OT, MOUTHWASH, T

87. MUSIC INSTRUMENTS

- CONDUCTOR
- XYLOPHONE
- OBOE
- CELLO
- FLUTE
- TAMBOURINE
- VIOLIN
- HARP
- KETTLE
- PIANO

88. THE LETTER "M"

- MAMMOTH
- MARMALADE
- MUSKET
- MARCH
- MOLE
- MONK
- MAMMAL (MA...)
- MYTH

89. MAKE-UP

- FOUNDATION
- KOHL
- BLUSH
- EYELINER
- LIPGLOSS
- MASCARA
- POWDER
- COSMETICS
- SHADOW
- BRUSHES

90. EXTREME SPORTS

- RAFTING
- BUNGEE
- SCUBA
- SKYDIVE
- ZORBING
- ANSWER / ...
- CLIMBING
- PARAGLIDE
- WINDSURF

91. MOVING HOUSE

- REMOVING
- RENT
- BOXES
- SIGN
- FURNITURE
- NEIGHBOR
- PACKING
- AGENT
- KEYS
- ADDRESS

92. AT THE ZOO

- ELEPHANT
- HIPPO
- TIGER
- TORTOISE
- PENGUIN
- RHINOCEROS
- MONKEY
- TARANTULA
- PANDA
- SNAKE

93. AT THE CIRCUS

- TOP
- CONIC / CON...
- APPLAUSE
- CLOWN
- RING
- SONY / ...
- NET
- ACROBAT
- TRAPEZE
- JUGGLER

94. ROYALTY

Q, C
GUARD, C, O
C, E, W
THRONE, W, N
R, N
O
PRINCESS
R, A, M
I, T, KINGDOM
N, K, O, A
CE, O
E, KNIGHTS

95. THE LETTER "P"

PHOTOGRAPH
I, R
N, PLUMBER
POEM, D
A, A, P, A
I, PAJAMAS, T
N, P, I, O
L, N, PORT
E, T
PEBBLES
R

96. FRUIT

P, CHERRY
E, A, L
BANANA, S, I
R, P, PLUM
G, P, B, E
R, L, E
STRAWBERRY, R
P, R
PEACH, Y
S

97. TRANSPORT

U
TANK, BUS
D, I
E, CAR
T, R, T, Y
R, G, A, C
A, R, X, L
MOTORBIKE
U, O
VAN, A
D, T

98. EMOTIONS

CROSS
C, A
CONFUSED
N, R, H
T, I, Y, T
E, G, I
N, HAPPY, R
T, T, E
EXCITED
N
RELAXED
D

99. THE LETTER "W"

W
WATERPROOF
A
WALTZ, WIDOW, W
I, H, A, A
N, E, L, T
D, WRINKLES, E
O, V, P, R
WIZARD, A, F
N, P, A
WATERWHEEL, L, L
R, L

100. FURNITURE

B
TA, U, C
U, N, H, D
BOOKCASE, R
N, BED, S
D, E
SHELVES
S, L, E
ROCKING, R
F, E
A, DRAWERS

101. DANCING

D
CONGA, A
O, N
PROMP, C
P, I
SPEAKERS, N
T, G
F, FRIDAY
L, T
O, LIGHTS
O, O
BREAKDANCE

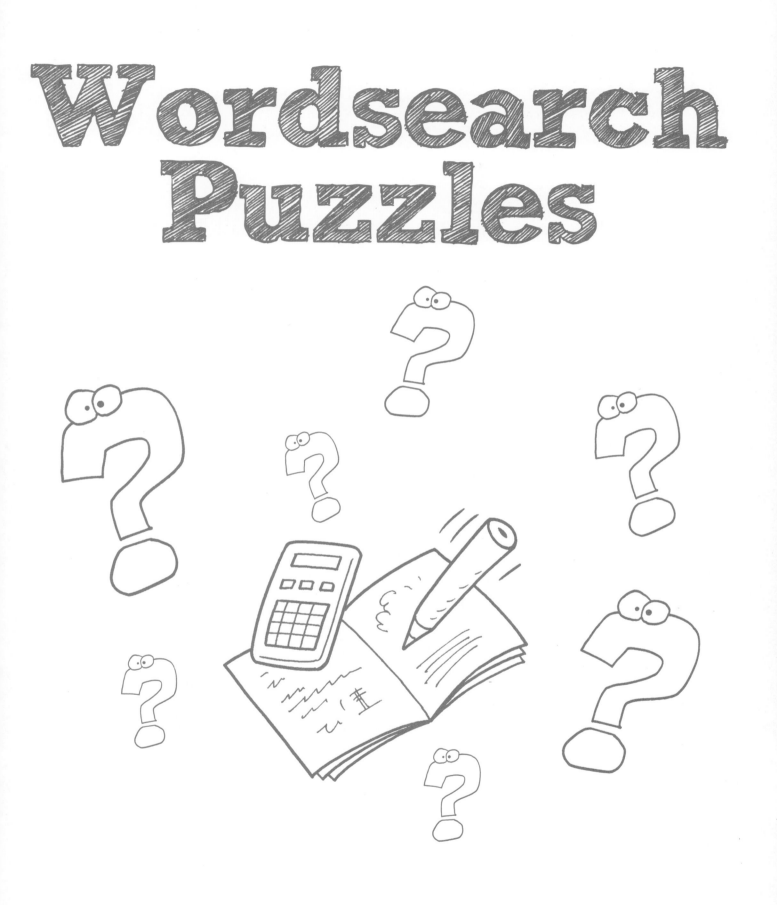

1. FISHY TAILS

Go fishing! How many can you catch?

CLAMS   LOBSTER   SCAMPI
COD   MACKEREL   SKATE
CRAB   MUSSELS   SOLE
HADDOCK   OYSTERS   SQUID
HAKE   PRAWNS   TURBOT
HERRING   SALMON

```
T P Y E H C Z S Q U I D
H R O A B A L O E H T L
H A D D O C K L W F F M
V W G N I R R E H C A L
S N R L O T O M Z C L E
E S A L M O N E L V X R
S M M O V J D S K A T E
M O T B E O B L S E I K
A D A S C A M P I N S C
L R G T U R B O T S T A
C S L E S S U M E I N M
F T S R E T S Y O R B D
```

2. DESSERT DELIGHT

There are plenty of desserts and pastries for you here!

CHEESECAKE   MERINGUE
CUSTARD   MOUSSE
FLAN   PIE
GATEAU   SEMOLINA
JELLO   SORBET   SUNDAE

```
C H E E S E C A K E J A
U N L S O T N G H C K C
S E M O L I N A T I I J
T A O B F T G H R R O O
A C U A E T A G I K F S
R S S C W C T S F L A N
D U S X O Z P O L A O L
E N E I E C E R E E G O
D D P C P K E B A V E L
Z A P P Y P I E W L P L
T E E A G E J T V M N E
F R M E R I N G U E W J
```

3. SUPERSTARS

Find the ten superstars hidden in the puzzle.

STARBURST   STARGAZE
STARDOM   STARLIGHT
STARDUST   STARRY
STARFISH   STARSHINE
STARFLOWER   STARSHIP

```
S T A R L I G H T A S C
T C G C K N V V A T T E
A E T H A M A S A S A H
R N P S T A R R Y T R A
B I A T O T F Y O A F W
U H R Z I I P Y O R L T
R S T T S S T A R D O M
S R Y H A R V E S U W O
T A P R O V I S T S E R
P T O P L A N S G T R N
C S T A R S H I P E D E
D A T E E Z A G R A T S
```

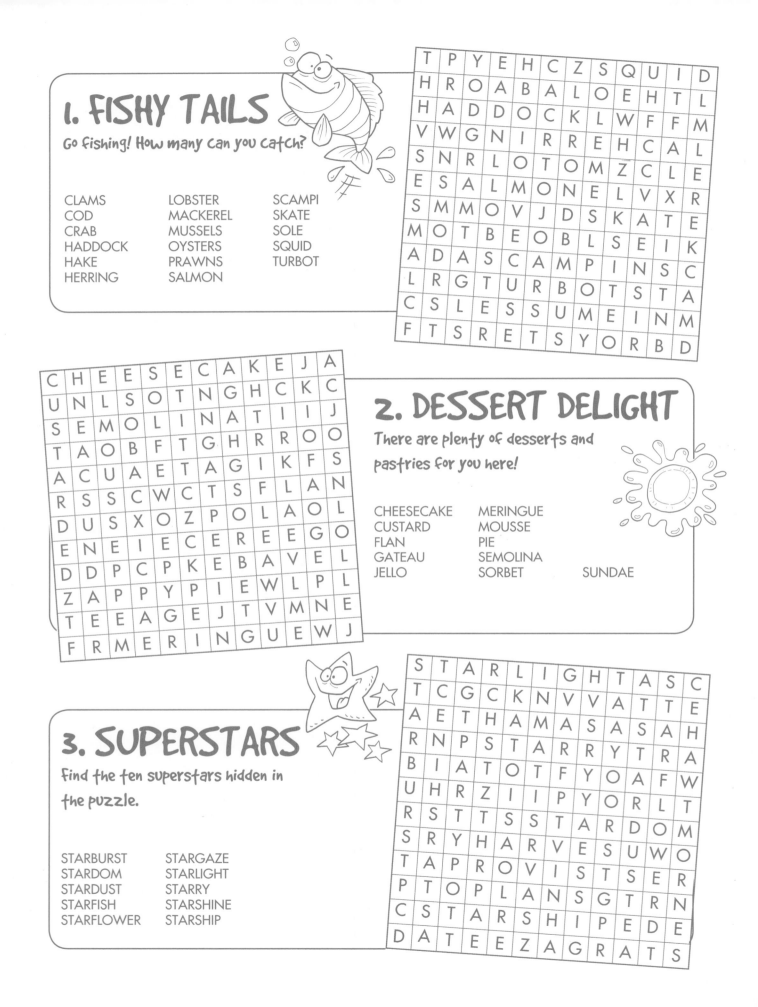

4. SPACE MISSION

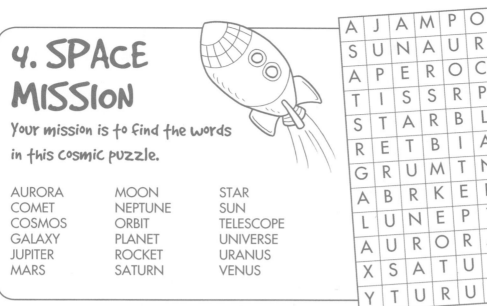

Your mission is to find the words in this cosmic puzzle.

AURORA
COMET
COSMOS
GALAXY
JUPITER
MARS

MOON
NEPTUNE
ORBIT
PLANET
ROCKET
SATURN

STAR
SUN
TELESCOPE
UNIVERSE
URANUS
VENUS

A	J	A	M	P	O	T	C	O	M	E	T
S	U	N	A	U	R	T	I	N	O	M	E
A	P	E	R	O	C	K	E	T	O	D	L
T	I	S	S	R	P	U	C	K	N	E	E
S	T	A	R	B	L	A	U	T	G	H	S
R	E	T	B	I	A	S	O	M	S	O	C
G	R	U	M	T	N	H	U	S	B	N	O
A	B	R	K	E	E	N	M	A	R	V	P
L	U	N	E	P	T	U	N	E	R	E	E
A	U	R	O	R	A	S	E	V	Y	N	M
X	S	A	T	U	S	U	N	A	R	U	E
Y	T	U	R	U	N	I	V	E	R	S	E

5. MAGIC WORDSEARCH

These words are linked to Halloween and magic!

ABRACADABRA
BROOM
CAULDRON
CHARM
CLOAK
DISAPPEAR

HALLOWEEN
MAGIC
POTION
PUMPKIN
SPELLS
TRICK

VANISH
WAND
WARLOCK
WISH
WITCH
WIZARD

P	K	H	S	L	L	E	P	S	H	A	R
H	C	A	U	L	D	R	O	N	R	V	Y
S	I	L	W	I	S	H	T	P	P	A	Z
I	R	L	O	N	E	C	I	G	A	M	P
N	T	O	A	V	B	R	O	O	M	O	U
A	Z	W	S	C	E	Y	N	Z	T	E	M
V	U	E	W	W	A	R	L	O	C	K	P
C	R	E	T	I	I	N	C	L	O	A	K
W	E	N	S	T	W	Z	O	O	P	A	I
A	B	R	A	C	A	D	A	B	R	A	N
N	A	R	C	H	A	R	M	R	B	C	L
D	I	S	A	P	P	E	A	R	D	D	E

6. SCHOOL IS COOL!

Have fun playing this school word puzzle.

ART
ASSEMBLY
BLACKBOARD
BOOKS
CALCULATOR
CHALK
CLASS
COMPUTER

CRAYONS
DESK
GRADES
HOMEWORK
MATH
PENCILS

PLAYGROUND
READING
TEACHER

O	X	C	C	U	H	T	A	M	A	R	W
L	C	A	L	C	U	L	A	T	O	R	I
D	O	E	A	R	A	O	S	S	R	E	B
E	M	M	S	A	C	C	S	V	A	H	L
K	P	A	S	Y	K	S	E	D	R	C	A
R	U	S	K	O	O	B	M	N	E	A	C
O	T	L	L	N	A	S	B	N	A	E	K
W	E	I	A	S	U	E	L	B	D	T	B
E	R	C	H	U	N	D	Y	P	I	O	O
M	A	N	C	T	R	A	R	T	N	O	A
O	L	E	Y	U	I	R	A	T	G	I	R
H	C	P	L	A	Y	G	R	O	U	N	D

7. WHAT'S THE BUZZ?

Find the noises animals and creatures make.

BARK
BELLOW
BLEAT
BUZZ
CACKLE
CHIRP
COO

GROWL
GRUNT
HISS
HOOT
HOWL
MOO
PURR

QUACK
SNARL
SNIFF
SNORT
SQUEAK
WARBLE
WOOF

```
P U Z I W O E L B R A W
B U Z Z E O F F R E D O
E T R G T K C A U Q A O
L C J R A A C R L T A F
L A I E E M O O W F E V
O C P W L S K S O F L E
W K R A B A W G R U N T
P L A P E S U N G H B T
Z E T U S N A R L E B R
Q U Q I P Y T O W A J O
A S N I F F T O O H O N
C H I R P F Y Q H I S S
```

8. HAUNTED HOUSE

Who is in the haunted house?

GARGOYLES
GHOSTS
GHOULS
MONSTERS

PHANTOMS
SKELETONS
SPECTERS
SPOOKS

VAMPIRES
WEREWOLF
ZOMBIES

```
G A R G O Y L E S P I E
H A P P A M S P O O K S
S O N E Y L I H P T O N
P S E R I P M A V S S M
E A Y R N T W N O S C O
C A L G H O S T S S A N
T T I H L Q W O E E R S
E C K O R O E M E I V T
R C E U O Q A S H B E E
S K M L W U L L K M C R
F T U S K E L E T O N S
F L O W E R E W A Z H P
```

9. TREASURE CHEST

What gems and jewels are hidden in the treasure chest?

AMBER
AMETHYST
BANGLE
BRACELET
CORAL
DIAMOND

EMERALD
JADE
NECKLACE
PENDANT
RING
RUBY

SAPPHIRE
TOPAZ
TURQUOISE
ZIRCON

```
D A Z Z A M E T H Y S T
R R Z A E K E G A N D U
U D I A M O N D S T O R
B R R P E L O N S N T Q
Y W C K R E B M A A O U
B C O C A S C O P D P O
A H N Z L G T L P N A I
N L O G D J N C H E Z S
G A V V S H E I I P A E
L R T E L E C A R B A T
E O A J M I N T E D A J
E C A L K C E N A C G O
```

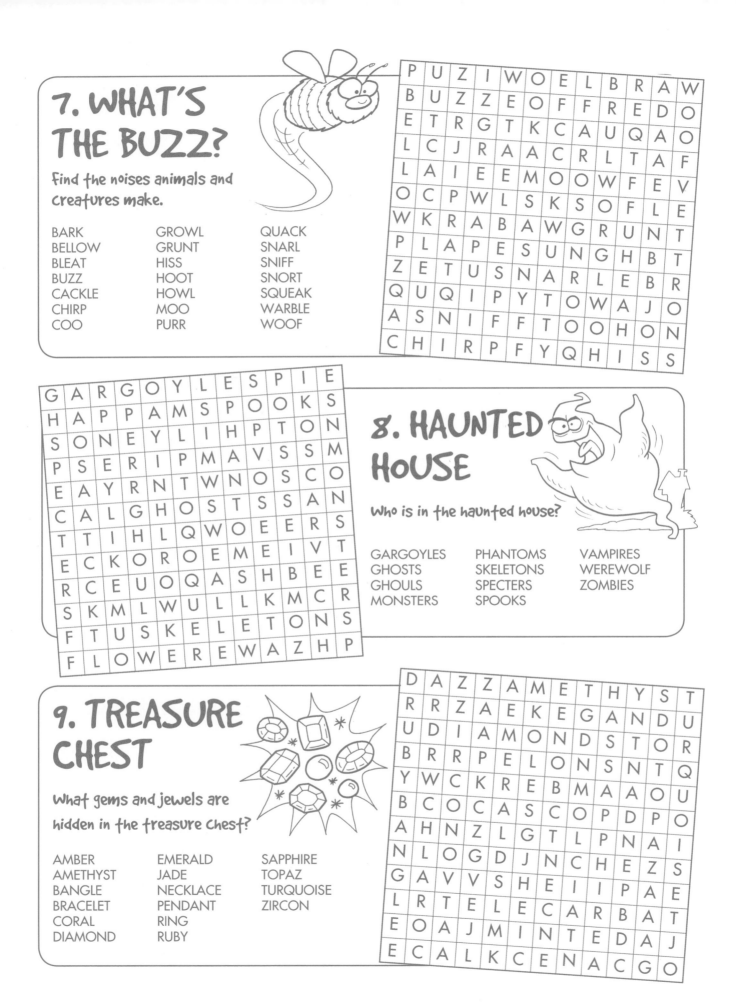

10. FAB FRUIT

Gather as many of these pieces of fruit as you can.

APRICOT
BANANA
CHERRY
DATES
GOOSEBERRY
GRAPES

KIWI
LEMON
MELON
ORANGE
PEACH
PEAR

PINEAPPLE
PLUM
RASPBERRY
STRAWBERRY

C	R	O	O	R	A	N	G	E	Y	E	S
H	A	B	A	N	A	N	A	A	T	L	T
E	S	N	O	O	R	Y	P	N	Q	P	R
R	E	J	O	V	A	R	B	W	Q	P	A
R	S	T	P	L	U	M	O	T	T	A	W
Y	R	R	E	B	E	S	O	O	G	E	B
S	H	R	A	N	O	M	E	L	D	N	E
C	A	G	R	A	P	E	S	O	F	I	R
I	W	I	K	I	R	I	W	I	R	P	R
F	A	T	R	A	S	P	B	E	R	R	Y
T	O	C	I	R	P	A	A	R	H	A	Y
D	P	E	A	C	H	S	E	T	A	D	O

11. COLOR CRAZY

All these words are brightly colored!

BALLOONS
CARNIVAL
CLOWN
CRAYONS
FIREWORKS
FRUIT

GEMS
MARBLES
NEON
PAINTS
PARROT
RAINBOW

SUNRISE
SUNSET

F	R	O	L	L	A	V	I	N	R	A	C
I	J	E	E	S	W	O	B	N	I	A	R
R	A	M	C	S	C	R	F	T	E	D	A
E	B	A	Q	D	G	E	M	S	S	E	Y
W	M	R	U	C	A	T	H	U	H	H	O
O	T	B	A	L	L	O	O	N	S	T	N
R	O	L	E	O	J	R	G	R	O	O	S
K	M	E	R	W	T	R	C	I	T	H	O
S	A	S	E	N	H	A	H	S	U	O	M
R	S	T	N	I	A	P	I	E	P	O	C
I	F	W	H	H	F	W	L	N	E	O	N
T	E	S	N	U	S	F	R	U	I	T	S

12. CANDY STORE

Seek the treats inside the candy store.

CANDY
CARAMELS
CHEWS
CHOCOLATE
FUDGE
GUMDROPS

LOLLIPOPS
MARSHMALLOW
MINTS
SHERBET
TOFFEE

C	A	N	D	Y	B	R	L	Y	T	L	S
A	E	T	T	E	B	R	E	H	S	O	L
R	I	U	Q	C	E	K	I	T	S	L	I
A	S	G	U	M	D	R	O	P	S	L	C
M	X	R	T	I	A	R	T	W	O	I	O
E	F	T	F	N	S	E	H	N	C	P	R
L	G	O	S	T	H	C	C	S	S	O	I
S	V	F	I	S	M	M	S	S	V	P	C
I	X	F	R	S	N	B	B	W	O	S	C
E	J	E	G	D	U	F	O	S	E	Z	E
G	U	E	E	T	A	L	O	C	O	H	C
M	A	R	S	H	M	A	L	L	O	W	C

13. FLOWER GARDEN

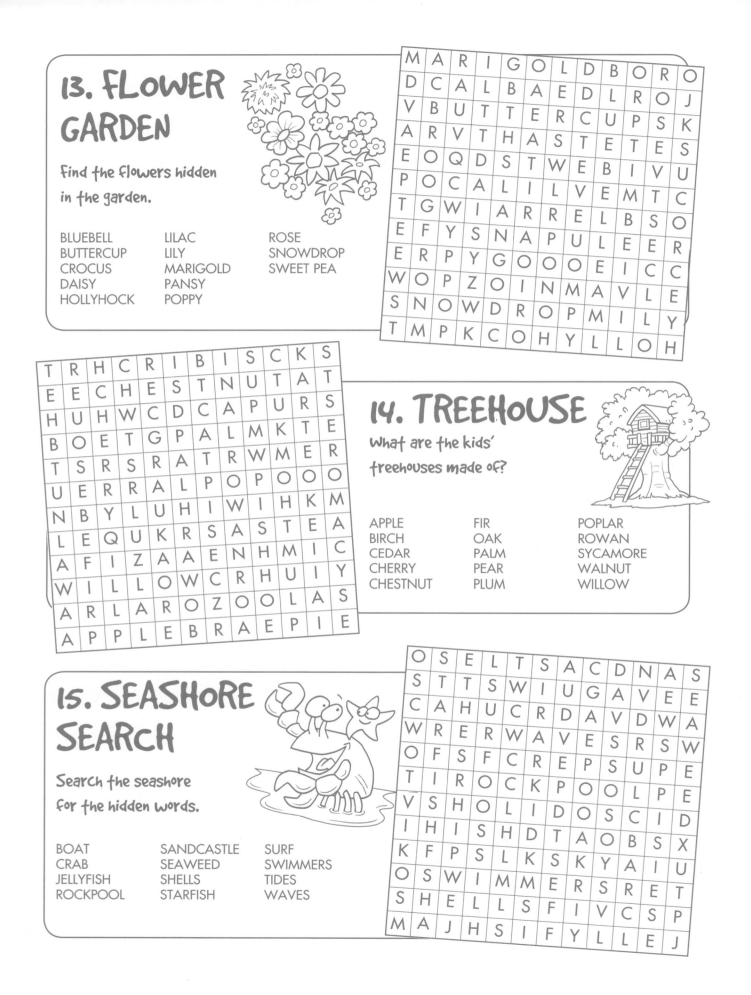

Find the flowers hidden in the garden.

BLUEBELL
BUTTERCUP
CROCUS
DAISY
HOLLYHOCK

LILAC
LILY
MARIGOLD
PANSY
POPPY

ROSE
SNOWDROP
SWEET PEA

M	A	R	I	G	O	L	D	B	O	R	O
D	C	A	L	B	A	E	D	L	R	O	J
V	B	U	T	T	E	R	C	U	P	S	K
A	R	V	T	H	A	S	T	E	T	E	S
E	O	Q	D	S	T	W	E	B	I	V	U
P	O	C	A	L	I	L	V	E	M	T	C
T	G	W	I	A	R	R	E	L	B	S	O
E	F	Y	S	N	A	P	U	L	E	E	R
E	R	P	Y	G	O	O	O	E	I	C	C
W	O	P	Z	O	I	N	M	A	V	L	E
S	N	O	W	D	R	O	P	M	I	L	Y
T	M	P	K	C	O	H	Y	L	L	O	H

14. TREEHOUSE

What are the kids' treehouses made of?

APPLE
BIRCH
CEDAR
CHERRY
CHESTNUT

FIR
OAK
PALM
PEAR
PLUM

POPLAR
ROWAN
SYCAMORE
WALNUT
WILLOW

T	R	H	C	R	I	B	I	S	C	K	S
E	E	C	H	E	S	T	N	U	T	A	T
H	U	H	W	C	D	C	A	P	U	R	S
B	O	E	T	G	P	A	L	M	K	T	E
T	S	R	S	R	A	T	R	W	M	E	R
U	E	R	R	A	L	P	O	P	O	O	O
N	B	Y	L	U	H	I	W	I	H	K	M
L	E	Q	U	K	R	S	A	S	T	E	A
A	F	I	Z	A	A	E	N	H	M	I	C
W	I	L	L	O	W	C	R	H	U	I	Y
A	R	L	A	R	O	Z	O	O	L	A	S
A	P	P	L	E	B	R	A	E	P	I	E

15. SEASHORE SEARCH

Search the seashore for the hidden words.

BOAT
CRAB
JELLYFISH
ROCKPOOL

SANDCASTLE
SEAWEED
SHELLS
STARFISH

SURF
SWIMMERS
TIDES
WAVES

O	S	E	L	T	S	A	C	D	N	A	S
S	T	T	S	W	I	U	G	A	V	E	E
C	A	H	U	C	R	D	A	V	D	W	A
W	R	E	R	W	A	V	E	S	R	S	W
O	F	S	F	C	R	E	P	S	U	P	E
T	I	R	O	C	K	P	O	O	L	P	E
V	S	H	O	L	I	D	O	S	C	I	D
I	H	I	S	H	D	T	A	O	B	S	X
K	F	P	S	L	K	S	K	Y	A	I	U
O	S	W	I	M	M	E	R	S	R	E	T
S	H	E	L	L	S	F	I	V	C	S	P
M	A	J	H	S	I	F	Y	L	L	E	J

16. WILD WEATHER

What's hidden in the weather chart?

CLOUDY	HAZY	
COOL	HOT	
CYCLONE	HURRICANE	SNOW
FREEZING	ICY	THUNDER
FOG	LIGHTNING	TORNADO
FROST	MIST	WET
HAILSTORM	RAIN	WINDY

```
H U R R I C A N E R R F
A C Y C L O N E R D T R
I S O W O R D C A S S E
L T R O R I B C I V E E
S N O W L Y B M N W R Z
T O R N A D O B C E E I
O S D E J N U H O T D N
R D B R O I H A P E N G
M B C V F W P Z I O U Z
M Y D U O L C Y W I H S
I C A C G L F R O S T S
L I G H T N I N G O G G
```

17. FUNNY WORDS

Enjoy searching for these humorous words.

CARTOON	HOWL	SNIGGER
COMEDY	HUMOROUS	WIT
FUNNY	JEST	
GAG	JOKE	
GIGGLE	LAUGH	
HILARIOUS	PUN	

```
S N I G G E R H G A G C
W A V E R C C A Y K I T
E W K A L A J O K E S E
L A U G H T E P T U U M
T I W I V B S Z L W O H
R C W G B O T Q M K R Y
A L Y G I C A R T O O N
H E N L J X D O Y R M U
C O M E D Y J J E A U P
A V L O Z Y N N U F H M
B R I D A Y L R O R F N
Y S U O I R A L I H J O
```

18. ANIMALS

Can you find the hiding animals?

CAT	LAMBS
CHICKENS	MICE
COW	PIG
DOG	RABBITS
DONKEY	RATS
DUCKS	SHEEP
GEESE	
GOATS	
HAMSTER	
HORSE	

```
S T S C C G H E O O P V
T A H D O G S Y T T L A
I R E I W R A E S R O H
B V E T H D E K O P C A
B E P I G I R N U I N M
A V C A M O T O A R V S
R R E A X S T D F C A T
E Y S N E K C I H C S E
S S K C U D H S R O U R
O Z E H F S B M A L A M
M I C E I L A T T E Y P
P R O G G O A T S N Q M
```

19. TOYS!

See how many toys you can find.

BALL
BAT
BICYCLE
BOAT
CRAYONS

DOLL
GAMES
KITE
PAINTS
RATTLE

SKATES
TRAIN
YOYO

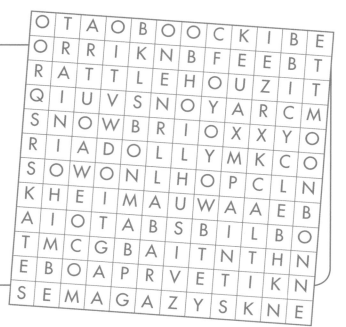

O	T	A	O	B	O	O	C	K	I	B	E
O	R	R	I	K	N	B	F	E	E	B	T
R	A	T	T	L	E	H	O	U	Z	I	T
Q	I	U	V	S	N	O	Y	A	R	C	M
S	N	O	W	B	R	I	O	X	X	Y	O
R	I	A	D	O	L	L	Y	M	K	C	O
S	O	W	O	N	L	H	O	P	C	L	N
K	H	E	I	M	A	U	W	A	A	E	B
A	I	O	T	A	B	S	B	I	L	B	O
T	M	C	G	B	A	I	T	N	T	H	N
E	B	O	A	P	R	V	E	T	I	K	N
S	E	M	A	G	A	Z	Y	S	K	N	E

20. GROCERY STORE

Can you find the items hidden in the store?

BACON
BEANS
BREAD
BUTTER
CHEESE
COFFEE
COOKIES

EGGS
JAM
MARGARINE
MARMALADE
MILK
PEPPER
SOUP

SUGAR
TEA

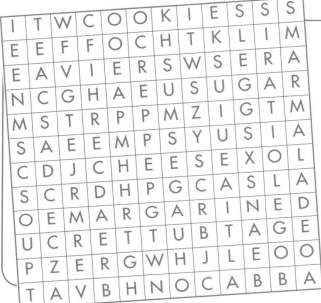

I	T	W	C	O	O	K	I	E	S	S	S
E	E	F	F	O	C	H	T	K	L	I	M
E	A	V	I	E	R	S	W	S	E	R	A
N	C	G	H	A	E	U	S	U	G	A	R
M	S	T	R	P	P	M	Z	I	G	T	M
S	A	E	E	M	P	S	Y	U	S	I	A
C	D	J	C	H	E	E	S	E	X	O	L
S	C	R	D	H	P	G	C	A	S	L	A
O	E	M	A	R	G	A	R	I	N	E	D
U	C	R	E	T	T	U	B	T	A	G	E
P	Z	E	R	G	W	H	J	L	E	O	O
T	A	V	B	H	N	O	C	A	B	B	A

21. VEGETABLE PATCH

Find the selection of vegetables here.

ARTICHOKE
BEET
BROCCOLI
CABBAGE
CARROT
CAULIFLOWER

KALE
LEEKS
ONION
POTATOES
SPINACH
SPROUTS

SQUASH
ZUCCHINI

J	E	Z	U	C	C	H	I	N	I	V	E
O	E	R	T	S	Q	U	A	S	H	I	R
F	S	S	K	A	L	E	F	R	E	D	E
E	I	L	O	C	C	O	R	B	O	E	W
S	S	E	D	E	A	U	O	A	L	N	O
E	P	G	A	A	R	W	N	O	D	J	L
O	I	A	B	U	R	N	I	P	C	E	F
T	N	B	E	L	O	Z	O	O	E	Q	I
A	A	B	E	T	T	K	N	K	B	X	L
T	C	A	T	F	F	J	S	F	B	S	U
O	H	C	E	K	O	H	C	I	T	R	A
P	A	S	T	U	O	R	P	S	Z	X	C

22. OCEANS AND SEAS

Go sailing! Find the oceans and seas in the grid.

ADRIATIC BLACK NORTH
ARCTIC CARIBBEAN PACIFIC
ATLANTIC CASPIAN RED
ANTARCTIC DEAD
BALTIC INDIAN

D	E	R	A	H	O	U	B	L	A	C	K
R	E	F	B	I	A	T	E	R	R	T	G
E	C	A	S	P	I	A	N	O	C	H	P
F	I	T	C	P	P	U	F	W	T	I	A
C	T	L	D	J	I	V	G	L	I	P	C
I	L	A	E	K	E	W	A	K	C	N	I
T	A	N	T	A	R	C	T	I	C	A	F
A	B	T	F	L	Q	X	G	D	M	I	I
I	D	I	K	M	R	Y	I	A	A	D	C
R	E	C	A	R	I	B	B	E	A	N	L
D	V	U	G	N	S	Z	J	D	W	I	N
A	T	H	T	R	O	N	K	T	I	M	O

23. WHAT'S IN THE BATHROOM?

How many things can you find in the bathroom?

BUBBLE BATH SHOWER TOILET
FAUCET SINK TOOTHBRUSH
MAT SOAP TOOTHPASTE
MIRROR SPONGE TOWEL
SHAMPOO TILES

T	H	I	M	B	L	V	K	N	I	S	U
O	S	E	L	I	T	E	W	S	T	P	Q
P	U	R	R	S	H	A	M	P	O	O	H
H	R	Q	U	H	S	A	U	R	I	N	T
O	B	W	S	O	A	P	T	S	L	G	A
R	H	W	R	W	A	N	T	I	E	E	B
D	T	O	W	E	L	C	H	I	T	G	E
E	O	E	D	R	L	H	A	F	U	O	L
N	O	F	A	U	C	E	T	G	H	I	B
T	T	O	O	T	H	P	A	S	T	E	B
A	C	A	T	Y	H	O	T	F	A	U	U
M	I	R	R	O	R	F	A	T	B	O	B

24. WHAT'S IN THE KITCHEN?

How many things can you find in the kitchen?

BLENDER OVEN STOVE
FREEZER PANS TOASTER
GRILL POTS
KETTLE REFRIGERATOR
MICROWAVE SINK

R	O	L	P	D	O	T	R	I	F	E	C
E	V	S	T	O	V	E	E	B	R	I	I
F	E	K	P	K	E	E	D	E	E	A	N
R	P	C	I	O	N	S	N	L	E	L	K
I	I	W	J	S	E	R	E	A	Z	H	A
G	N	P	G	R	I	L	L	C	E	O	Y
E	C	O	J	P	U	T	B	K	R	B	L
R	E	T	S	A	O	T	O	P	P	U	S
A	C	S	S	N	O	T	H	A	T	I	I
T	V	A	R	S	S	G	E	H	E	R	N
O	X	I	I	P	E	E	L	T	T	E	K
R	Z	E	V	A	W	O	R	C	I	M	K

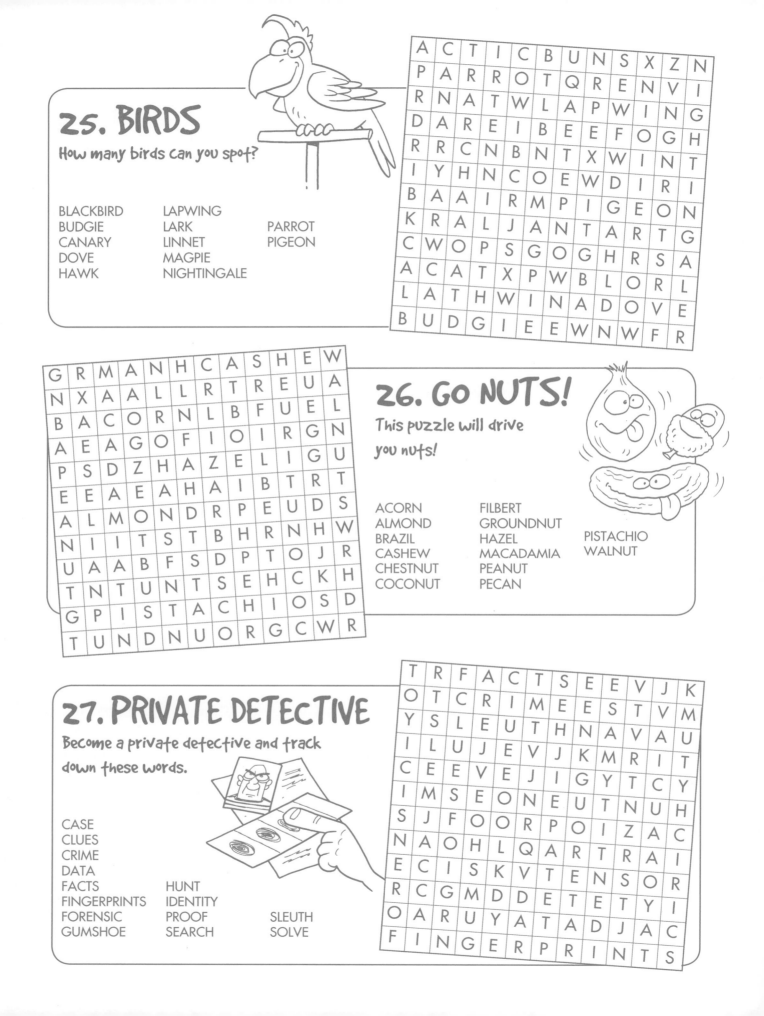

25. BIRDS

How many birds can you spot?

A	C	T	I	C	B	U	N	S	X	Z	N
P	A	R	R	O	T	Q	R	E	N	V	I
R	N	A	T	W	L	A	P	W	I	N	G
D	A	R	E	I	B	E	E	F	O	G	H
R	R	C	N	B	N	T	X	W	I	N	T
I	Y	H	N	C	O	E	W	D	I	R	I
B	A	A	I	R	M	P	I	G	E	O	N
K	R	A	L	J	A	N	T	A	R	T	G
C	W	O	P	S	G	O	G	H	R	S	A
A	C	A	T	X	P	W	B	L	O	R	L
L	A	T	H	W	I	N	A	D	O	V	E
B	U	D	G	I	E	E	W	N	W	F	R

BLACKBIRD
BUDGIE
CANARY
DOVE
HAWK

LAPWING
LARK
LINNET
MAGPIE
NIGHTINGALE

PARROT
PIGEON

26. GO NUTS!

This puzzle will drive you nuts!

G	R	M	A	N	H	C	A	S	H	E	W
N	X	A	A	L	L	R	T	R	E	U	A
B	A	C	O	R	N	L	B	F	U	E	L
A	E	A	G	O	F	I	O	I	R	G	N
P	S	D	Z	H	A	Z	E	L	I	G	U
E	E	A	E	A	H	A	I	B	T	R	T
A	L	M	O	N	D	R	P	E	U	D	S
N	I	I	T	S	T	B	H	R	N	H	W
U	A	A	B	F	S	D	P	T	O	J	R
T	N	T	U	N	T	S	E	H	C	K	H
G	P	I	S	T	A	C	H	I	O	S	D
T	U	N	D	N	U	O	R	G	C	W	R

ACORN
ALMOND
BRAZIL
CASHEW
CHESTNUT
COCONUT

FILBERT
GROUNDNUT
HAZEL
MACADAMIA
PEANUT
PECAN

PISTACHIO
WALNUT

27. PRIVATE DETECTIVE

Become a private detective and track down these words.

T	R	F	A	C	T	S	E	E	V	J	K
O	T	C	R	I	M	E	E	S	T	V	M
Y	S	L	E	U	T	H	N	A	V	A	U
I	L	U	J	E	V	J	K	M	R	I	T
C	E	E	V	E	J	I	G	Y	T	C	Y
I	M	S	E	O	N	E	U	T	N	U	H
S	J	F	O	O	R	P	O	I	Z	A	C
N	A	O	H	L	Q	A	R	T	R	A	I
E	C	I	S	K	V	T	E	N	S	O	R
R	C	G	M	D	D	E	T	E	T	Y	I
O	A	R	U	Y	A	T	A	D	J	A	C
F	I	N	G	E	R	P	R	I	N	T	S

CASE
CLUES
CRIME
DATA
FACTS
FINGERPRINTS
FORENSIC
GUMSHOE

HUNT
IDENTITY
PROOF
SEARCH

SLEUTH
SOLVE

28. ROBOTS

Find the words linked to robots.

ANDROID
COMPUTER
CONTROLS
CYBORG
FUTURISTIC
HUMANOID
INTELLIGENCE
MACHINE
MEMORY
PROCESS
PROGRAM
ROBOT
TECHNOLOGY

```
S H I S L O R T N O C S
P T E C H N O L O G Y S
D V N O U F B H E R B E
V N I M H G O H O R O C
H K H P S D T M A X R O
U W C U E C E B A R G R
M S A T D M A R G O R P
A X M E C I T E R E U E
N I D R B J U N E I E J
O E C I T S I R U T U F
I N T E L L I G E N C E
D I O R D N A S T E R Z
```

29. AROUND THE WORLD

Find the continents and countries in the puzzle.

AFRICA
AMERICA
AUSTRALIA
BELGIUM
BRITAIN
CHINA
EGYPT
FRANCE
GERMANY
ICELAND
ITALY
JAPAN
NORWAY
RUSSIA
SPAIN
SWEDEN

```
S P A I N Y I N A P A J
W K I C O M M M J F M R
E E S E S O U S X E E D
D C S L P N I A T I R B
E D U A L O G H P W I U
N S R N A R L O Y A C Z
E C M D V W E U G C A E
C H O A C A B S E I S S
N I T A L Y E E V R R C
A N D R H I T R E F R I
R A U S T R A L I A I C
F R O I L Y N A M R E G
```

30. GLOBE TROTTERS

Can you find these countries?

AUSTRIA
BRAZIL
CANADA
DENMARK
FINLAND
GREECE
GREENLAND
HOLLAND
HUNGARY
INDIA
MEXICO
PERU
PORTUGAL
SWITZERLAND
THAILAND
TURKEY

```
I A V A L L C A N A D A
N H M E X I C O F I N U
D U Y O R Z N R O B A S
I N E K R A M N E D L T
A G K G R R E A T N R R
X A R E X B W D H A E I
E R U T D F E Z A L Z A
C Y T R U E T E I N T R
E P O R T U G A L I I V
E Q E R C V G H A F W A
R P C H O L L A N D S L
G R E E N L A N D J R O
```

31. CREEPY-CRAWLY

This puzzle is full of creepy-crawly creatures.

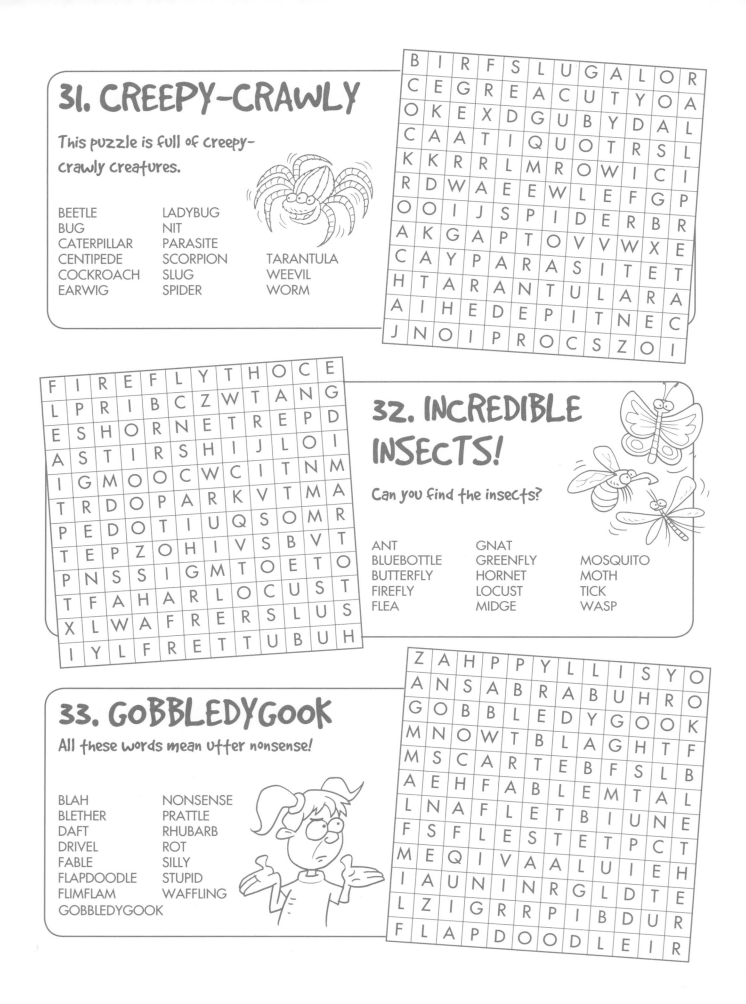

BEETLE
BUG
CATERPILLAR
CENTIPEDE
COCKROACH
EARWIG

LADYBUG
NIT
PARASITE
SCORPION
SLUG
SPIDER

TARANTULA
WEEVIL
WORM

```
B I R F S L U G A L O R
C E G R E A C U T Y O A
O K E X D G U B Y D A L
C A A T I Q U O T R S L
K K R R L M R O W I C I
R D W A E E W L E F G P
O O I J S P I D E R B R
A K G A P T O V V W X E
C A Y P A R A S I T E T
H T A R A N T U L A R A
A I H E D E P I T N E C
J N O I P R O C S Z O I
```

32. INCREDIBLE INSECTS!

Can you find the insects?

ANT
BLUEBOTTLE
BUTTERFLY
FIREFLY
FLEA

GNAT
GREENFLY
HORNET
LOCUST
MIDGE

MOSQUITO
MOTH
TICK
WASP

```
F I R E F L Y T H O C E
L P R I B C Z W T A N G
E S H O R N E T R E P D
A S T I R S H I J L O I
I G M O O C W C I T N M
T R D O P A R K V T M A
P E D O T I U Q S O M R
T E P Z O H I V S B V T
P N S S I G M T O E T O
T F A H A R L O C U S T
X L W A F R E R S L U S
I Y L F R E T T U B U H
```

33. GOBBLEDYGOOK

All these words mean utter nonsense!

BLAH
BLETHER
DAFT
DRIVEL
FABLE
FLAPDOODLE
FLIMFLAM
GOBBLEDYGOOK

NONSENSE
PRATTLE
RHUBARB
ROT
SILLY
STUPID
WAFFLING

```
Z A H P P Y L L I S Y O
A N S A B R A B U H R O
G O B B L E D Y G O O K
M N O W T B L A G H T F
M S C A R T E B F S L B
A E H F A B L E M T A L
L N A F L E T B I U N E
F S F L E S T E T P C T
M E Q I V A A L U I E H
I A U N I N R G L D T E
L Z I G R R P I B D U R
F L A P D O O D L E I R
```

34. MUSICAL INSTRUMENTS

Can you fnd the instruments?

BAGPIPES
BANJO
BELLS
FLUTE
GUITAR
HARMONICA

KAZOO
KEYBOARD
OBOE
PIANO
RECORDER
TAMBOURINE

VIOLA
VIOLIN

B	R	I	P	J	U	S	O	O	Z	A	K
A	G	U	I	T	A	R	S	R	I	E	E
C	T	N	A	A	R	U	O	E	P	N	Y
I	E	R	N	W	T	L	I	D	M	I	B
N	I	L	O	I	V	E	L	R	W	R	O
O	R	A	I	T	I	S	R	O	Q	U	A
M	B	A	N	J	O	O	L	C	U	O	R
R	E	O	D	F	L	U	T	E	O	B	D
A	L	R	E	F	A	Y	R	R	I	M	R
H	L	U	T	E	I	T	G	N	S	A	A
L	S	V	E	S	H	O	P	I	E	T	T
O	S	C	S	E	P	I	P	G	A	B	H

35. "A" WORDS

All these words start
with the letter A.

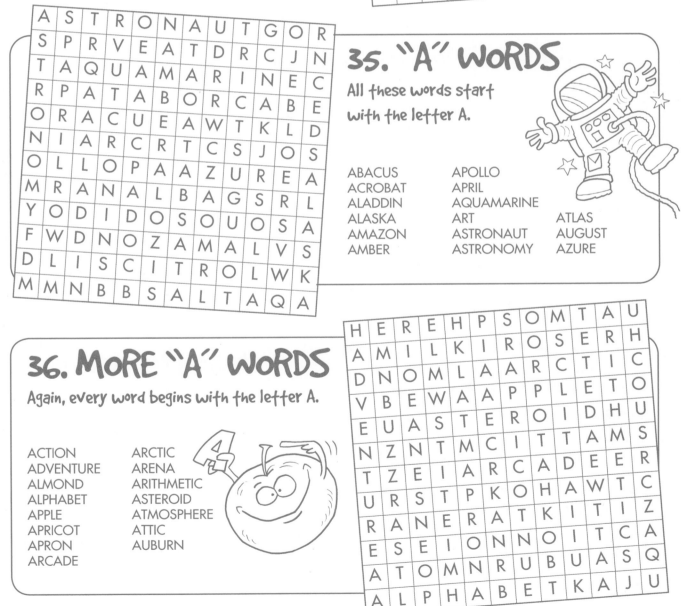

ABACUS
ACROBAT
ALADDIN
ALASKA
AMAZON
AMBER

APOLLO
APRIL
AQUAMARINE
ART
ASTRONAUT
ASTRONOMY

ATLAS
AUGUST
AZURE

A	S	T	R	O	N	A	U	T	G	O	R
S	P	R	V	E	A	T	D	R	C	J	N
T	A	Q	U	A	M	A	R	I	N	E	C
R	P	A	T	A	B	O	R	C	A	B	E
O	R	A	C	U	E	A	W	T	K	L	D
N	I	A	R	C	R	T	C	S	J	O	S
O	L	L	O	P	A	A	Z	U	R	E	A
M	R	A	N	A	L	B	A	G	S	R	L
Y	O	D	I	D	O	S	O	U	O	S	A
F	W	D	N	O	Z	A	M	A	L	V	S
D	L	I	S	C	I	T	R	O	L	W	K
M	M	N	B	B	S	A	L	T	A	Q	A

36. MORE "A" WORDS

Again, every word begins with the letter A.

ACTION
ADVENTURE
ALMOND
ALPHABET
APPLE
APRICOT
APRON
ARCADE

ARCTIC
ARENA
ARITHMETIC
ASTEROID
ATMOSPHERE
ATTIC
AUBURN

H	E	R	E	H	P	S	O	M	T	A	U
A	M	I	L	K	I	R	O	S	E	R	H
D	N	O	M	L	A	A	R	C	T	I	C
V	B	E	W	A	A	P	P	L	E	T	O
E	U	A	S	T	E	R	O	I	D	H	U
N	Z	N	T	M	C	I	T	T	A	M	S
T	Z	E	I	A	R	C	A	D	E	E	R
U	R	S	T	P	K	O	H	A	W	T	C
R	A	N	E	R	A	T	K	I	T	I	Z
E	S	E	I	O	N	N	O	I	T	C	A
A	T	O	M	N	R	U	B	U	A	S	Q
A	L	P	H	A	B	E	T	K	A	J	U

37. BIRTHDAYS!

All these words are associated with birthdays.

CAKE
CANDLES
CELEBRATE
DANCING
DECORATIONS
FRIENDS
FUN
GAMES
GIFTS
HAPPY
HATS
ICING
MUSIC
PARTY
PRESENTS
SINGING
WISH

38. DOGS

Find the dogs in the word puzzle.

BASSET
BEAGLE
CHOW
CORGI
DACHSHUND
DOBERMAN
LABRADOR
PEKINESE
POMERANIAN
ROTTWEILER
SETTER
SHEEPDOG
WOLFHOUND

39. MORE DOGS

Discover the dogs hidden here.

AIREDALE
BLOODHOUND
BOXER
BULLDOG
CHIHUAHUA
COLLIE
DALMATIAN
GREYHOUND
HUSKY
NEWFOUNDLAND
POODLE
PUG
SPANIEL
WHIPPET

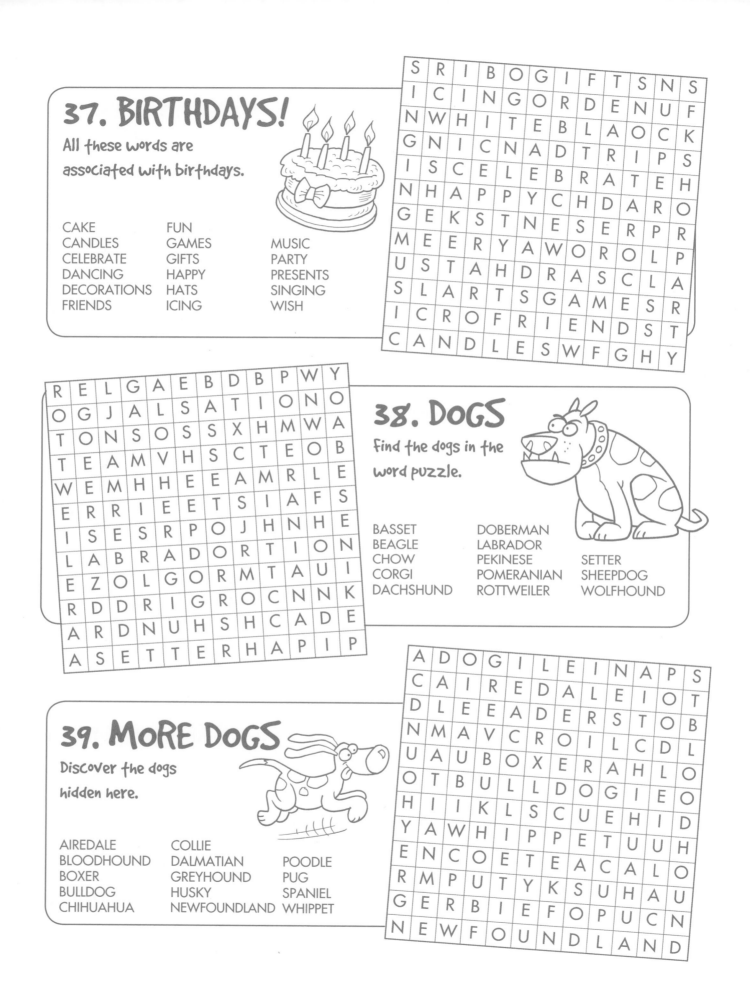

40. TRAIN STATION

Find the words associated with train stations.

BUFFERS
CARRIAGES
DRIVER
GUARD
PASSENGERS

PLATFORM
RAILS
SHUNTER
SIGNALS
SLEEPER

TICKETS
TIMETABLE
WHISTLE

B	S	E	G	A	I	R	R	A	C	H	W
R	E	A	D	S	T	E	K	C	I	T	H
S	D	R	I	V	E	R	I	V	A	I	I
R	E	E	A	W	I	F	E	A	L	M	S
E	A	P	S	I	G	N	A	L	S	E	T
F	V	E	E	I	L	D	R	O	J	T	L
F	I	E	S	T	B	S	D	E	P	A	E
U	P	L	A	T	F	O	R	M	D	B	P
B	D	S	U	N	N	E	A	W	S	L	P
A	S	U	R	E	T	N	U	H	S	E	A
W	O	R	G	H	O	R	G	S	Q	U	I
T	A	S	R	E	G	N	E	S	S	A	P

41. SOCCER CRAZY

Search for the soccer words.

BALL
CORNER
DRAW
GOAL
FLAG
FOUL
KICK

MANAGER
NETS
REFEREE
RELEGATION
SAVE
SCORE
SOCCER

SUBSTITUTE
TACKLE
TEAM

R	S	T	B	S	L	C	O	R	N	E	R
I	M	A	E	T	U	H	U	E	D	S	E
T	L	C	W	E	V	Z	O	F	O	U	L
L	M	K	I	N	E	N	E	E	R	B	E
I	R	L	H	T	M	W	A	R	D	S	G
K	A	E	I	I	A	A	R	E	B	T	A
E	T	F	K	N	N	S	H	E	O	I	T
E	D	T	O	S	A	E	J	T	R	T	I
V	F	F	L	A	G	C	I	K	A	U	O
A	E	A	R	E	E	R	O	C	S	T	N
S	O	C	C	E	R	B	K	I	N	E	A
G	E	K	N	R	A	S	E	K	E	Y	F

42. COWBOY RANCH

Find the ranching words.

BRONCO
CATTLE
CHAPS
COWBOY
HORSE
LARIAT
LASSO
PRAIRIE

RANCH
RANGER
SADDLE
SHEEP
SPURS
STETSON
TROUGH

R	E	G	N	A	R	D	R	H	A	W	R
A	S	C	A	R	F	B	R	O	N	C	O
R	T	R	U	E	B	E	X	R	I	O	U
S	E	I	R	I	A	R	P	S	E	V	J
T	R	O	U	G	H	V	E	E	A	C	B
E	E	C	A	T	T	L	E	L	G	F	E
T	W	O	D	B	A	V	H	O	U	S	A
S	E	W	I	S	O	B	S	R	E	S	H
O	I	B	S	V	P	L	S	P	A	H	C
N	E	O	A	E	V	U	P	A	R	K	N
S	D	Y	D	S	L	A	R	I	A	T	A
J	O	J	E	L	D	D	A	S	W	O	R

43. CIRCUS

Find the words linked to the circus.

ACROBAT
ACTS
CLOWNS
ELEPHANTS
HORSES

JUGGLE
LIONS
MAGIC
RIGGING
RING

SHOWS
TIGERS
TRAINER
TRAPEZE
TENT

```
E L G G U J I G Z I P Z
L W I P T R A P E Z E B
E C M A G I C R T D Y I
P J R F E N P J A C T S
H G N I G G I R B L E H
A S D F N E O F O O S O
N E O R D S B K R W U W
T S E S R O H Z C N J S
S A R E S D S T A S G K
R O G W J A E W E B E E
L I O N S R T Q V N F N
T R A I N E R R A R T O
```

44. COMPUTERS

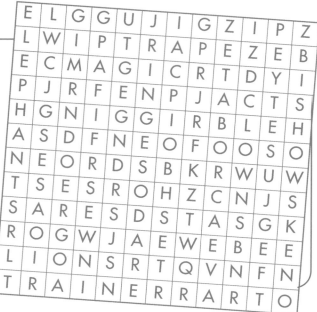

Use your skills to find the computer words.

COMPUTER
DESKTOP
DISK
FONT
GAMES
HARDWARE

KEYBOARD
INPUT
LAPTOP
MAIL
MEMORY
MODEM

MOUSE
NET
PRINTER
SOFTWARE
WEB

```
D E R D R A O B Y E K U
E I D R E T N I R P S D
S E V R R E S U O M I R
K R I F I F D Z M C D O
T C B I O S E U E R O H
O R A N V E S E M A G A
P O T P A L N H A M R R
R A I U T O I P Y E R D
T H W T T I T A E D G W
N Z B R E T U P M O C A
R E V L E M K L T M A R
W A T F S O F T W A R E
```

45. STAR SIGNS

Search for the star signs in this zodiac puzzle.

ARIES
AQUARIUS
BULL
CAPRICORN
CRAB
FISH
GEMINI

GOAT
LEO
LIBRA
LION
PISCES
RAM
SAGITTARIUS

SCORPIO
TAURUS
TWINS
VIRGO
ZODIAC

```
S C O R P I O T L A M D
A S A R D N W A R I E S
G O A T A I W U A Y O V
I E S E N M R R M T E N
T A V S L E P U H I L E
T A R F E G E S C L T P
A R B I L G R P A L E O
R E A S C O H I I U T G
I B R H W I J S D B O R
U U C A P R I C O R N I
S Q U E R T E E Z I S V
A Q U A R I U S H I P Y
```

46. HERBS

find the herbs hidden in the puzzle.

BASIL
BAY LEAF
CHERVIL
CHIVES
CORIANDER

DILL
FENNEL
MARJORAM
MINT
PARSLEY

ROSEMARY
SAGE
SAVORY
THYME

```
S E T A F A E L Y A B L
A M A R J O R A M C A R
L Y S P E P O R I C S O
R H S A T M A N N H I S
E T K I G M I X T E L E
D O F E X E E M J R K M
N R L E N N E F D V D A
A J L O E V A Z A I T R
I C I Q Z P A R S L E Y
R E D R L I F T E X E R
O S T S A V O R Y O U W
C H I V E S O N D A R O
```

```
S D R A C B S U V K A Y
V E A T R R E A K F A S
M C H R I S T M A S D S
I E Q E C E B D E R Y T
S M Y E R S C A R O L S
T B J T I M H N T A T D
L E K N H G I E L S N N
E R K A S R M A E S M A
T I L E P H N P S R W L
O U V N D F E V N F A R
E L H O L L Y D I Y I A
E D H S T D B S T F I G
```

47. CHRISTMAS

find these christmas time words.

CARDS
CAROLS
CHIMNEY
CHRISTMAS
DECEMBER
ELVES
GARLANDS

GIFTS
HOLLY
MISTLETOE
SLEIGH
TINSEL
TOYS
TREE

48. FESTIVE FUN

And these festive ones, too!

BAUBLES
CANDLES
CHESTNUTS
COLD
DECORATIONS
FAIRY
FEAST

LIGHTS
REINDEER
RUDOLPH
SANTA
SNOW
STAR
YULETIDE

```
R U D O L P H F A I R Y
E A R T C H J K E S W U
I F A V R T S T H G I L
N E V E Y J T S Z S H E
D S E L B U A B A T T T
E C R S I S R T N U A I
E H T F E A S T A N S D
R A T M E L E M O T N E
W T I F W M D S A S H U
O N C O L D B N M E F D
R A N F A D R D A H J K
K S N O I T A R O C E D
```

49. FIRE STATION

All the words here are linked to a fire station.

AXE
BELL
ENGINE
FIRE
FOAM

HELMETS
HOSE
LADDER
MASKS
POLE

RADIO
RESCUE
TURNTABLE
UNIFORM
WATER

W	O	F	F	U	N	I	F	O	R	M	I
D	R	A	I	T	E	R	E	T	A	W	I
A	R	K	O	R	I	F	T	C	D	O	D
J	O	N	R	S	E	C	B	L	I	V	E
E	L	O	P	S	L	V	R	E	O	S	N
F	A	A	S	L	B	E	L	L	A	K	T
O	D	L	O	S	A	R	A	H	S	S	R
R	D	T	B	O	T	I	C	B	T	A	E
E	E	N	G	I	N	E	H	U	O	M	S
S	R	D	D	N	R	A	S	T	A	G	C
H	E	A	R	Y	U	S	K	O	S	X	U
H	E	L	M	E	T	S	F	R	H	U	E

50. "B" WORDS

Find the words starting with the letter B.

BAMBOOZLE
BANANA
BAT
BAUBLE
BEAUTY
BEEHIVE
BILLION

BINOCULARS
BLOSSOM
BLUEBELL
BOAT
BONFIRE
BOOK
BOX

BOY
BREAD
BREAKFAST
BUBBLE
BUTTER
BUZZ

F	B	H	B	I	B	M	B	L	B	T	A
B	I	N	O	C	U	L	A	R	S	A	C
L	L	E	N	B	T	M	N	I	M	O	T
O	L	V	F	L	T	D	A	E	R	B	T
S	I	I	I	U	E	O	N	L	A	J	S
S	O	H	R	E	R	R	A	U	J	K	A
O	N	E	E	B	I	N	B	O	Y	Y	F
M	S	E	V	E	X	L	U	O	R	T	K
R	S	B	K	L	E	A	J	B	F	U	A
X	A	O	G	L	C	K	G	U	I	A	E
B	O	B	A	M	B	O	O	Z	L	E	R
B	U	B	B	L	E	V	R	Z	S	B	B

51. PUZZLE WORDS

All these words have something to do with puzzles.

ANSWER
CLUES
CODE
CRYPTIC
ENIGMA
GRID

JIGSAW
LOGIC
MAZE
MIND
MYSTERY
PUZZLE

RIDDLE
QUIZ
SOLUTIONS
WORDSEARCH

W	A	I	C	R	Y	P	T	I	C	R	O
O	K	E	J	C	R	U	Z	O	O	C	E
R	Y	N	A	R	A	Z	A	Q	U	I	Z
D	N	I	M	E	B	Z	X	G	D	G	A
S	R	G	R	W	A	L	C	L	U	O	M
E	R	M	Y	S	T	E	R	Y	F	L	A
A	A	A	A	N	E	J	I	G	S	A	W
R	H	Z	D	A	I	E	D	O	C	K	O
C	R	B	R	I	V	E	D	L	L	S	O
H	P	O	T	B	R	W	L	D	U	D	F
Q	U	E	O	M	I	G	E	W	E	R	I
A	S	N	O	I	T	U	L	O	S	O	H

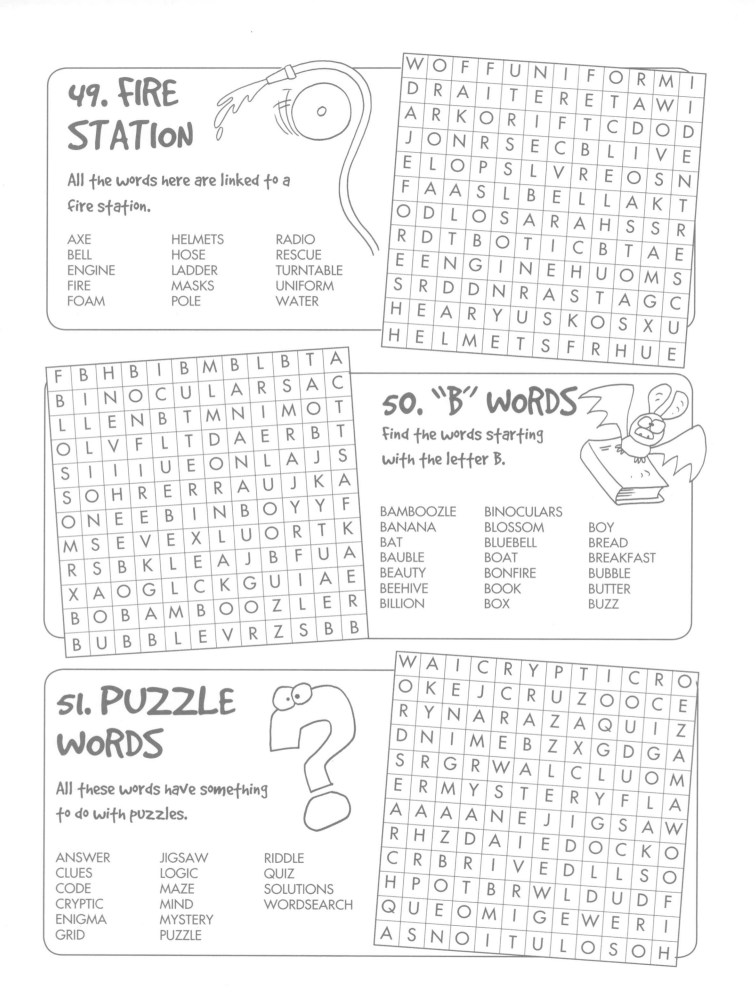

52. COOL!

This wordsearch is really cool.

ARCTIC
CHILLY
COLD
COOL
FREEZING
FROSTBITE

GLACIER
HAILSTONE
ICELAND
POLAR
SLEET
SNOWFLAKE

SNOWSTORM
WINTRY

I	C	H	I	L	L	Y	D	D	V	I	W
R	R	B	A	L	K	R	G	J	Y	C	I
I	A	S	N	O	W	F	L	A	K	E	N
R	L	N	I	U	N	R	L	R	O	L	T
C	O	O	E	C	O	O	L	C	A	A	R
S	P	W	V	O	Y	S	U	T	I	N	Y
T	E	S	I	L	J	T	R	I	O	D	E
E	D	T	H	D	N	B	I	C	T	L	L
E	N	O	T	S	L	I	A	H	V	E	A
L	J	R	N	I	O	T	R	H	X	S	E
S	T	M	I	O	R	E	I	C	A	L	G
B	R	U	E	G	N	I	Z	E	E	R	F

53. IT'S A JUNGLE!

Find the animals and creatures hidden here.

CHEETAH
CHIMP
COUGAR
GECKO
GIRAFFE

GORILLA
JAGUAR
MONKEY
MOSQUITO
PANTHER

TIGER
VIPER
VULTURE
ZEBRA

M	O	S	Q	U	I	T	O	L	D	G	W
O	S	T	K	T	A	K	W	I	W	O	I
N	O	R	T	K	C	A	J	K	E	R	F
K	V	T	I	E	E	F	F	A	R	I	G
E	I	H	G	R	H	O	L	R	O	L	E
Y	R	I	E	E	C	G	D	B	L	L	R
E	I	M	R	P	C	H	E	E	T	A	H
D	P	O	M	I	O	I	H	Z	U	S	W
A	C	I	F	V	U	L	T	U	R	E	H
D	H	U	S	A	G	I	R	I	L	P	A
C	R	P	A	J	A	G	U	A	R	Z	V
R	A	F	X	E	R	E	H	T	N	A	P

54. JUNGLE FUN!

Hunt for even more hidden animals and creatures.

ANTELOPE
APE
COBRA
CROCODILE
ELEPHANT
HIPPO
HYENA
LEOPARD

LION
OCELOT
PIRANHA
SNAKE
SPIDER
RHINO

S	A	N	D	S	R	U	C	O	B	R	A
P	I	R	A	N	H	A	R	D	A	X	X
I	A	R	V	A	E	D	O	N	I	H	R
D	G	H	H	K	J	T	C	S	H	L	O
E	O	A	M	E	D	B	O	P	P	I	H
R	R	N	O	O	Y	J	D	I	F	O	R
I	B	T	N	G	I	E	I	I	O	N	O
A	N	E	Y	H	L	S	L	D	C	Z	S
S	F	L	J	L	R	E	E	M	E	D	E
L	E	O	P	A	R	D	D	O	L	L	S
E	M	P	P	N	I	C	N	W	O	L	I
M	A	E	L	E	P	H	A	N	T	I	G

55. "C" WORDS

All these words begin with the letter C.

CAFE CARTOON CHOCOLATE
CALCULATOR CAT CINDERELLA
CALENDAR CAVE CINEMA
CARAMEL CHARM COCOA
CARAVAN CHEF COMET
CARNIVAL CHERRY CREAM

S	A	F	E	T	A	L	O	C	O	H	C	C
L	N	C	I	N	D	E	R	E	L	L	A	
A	C	A	A	H	O	U	S	E	E	R	L	
V	S	R	O	R	C	I	N	E	M	A	C	
I	T	A	E	T	T	A	K	T	A	C	U	
N	T	V	O	A	H	O	E	S	R	E	L	
R	J	A	T	C	M	M	O	A	A	V	A	
A	N	N	E	H	O	S	R	N	C	A	T	
C	A	N	D	C	L	C	U	A	Q	C	O	
D	Y	R	R	E	H	C	U	P	H	Q	R	
C	C	A	L	E	N	D	A	R	R	C	S	
D	T	E	F	A	C	S	T	O	T	Y	F	

56. "D" WORDS

Look for the words beginning with the letter D.

DAILY DATE
DAIRY DAZZLE
DAISY DECEMBER DOVE
DANCE DESSERT DRAWING
DANDELION DINOSAUR DUCK
DARK DOODLE DYNAMIC

S	E	L	Z	Z	A	D	F	R	E	S	I
E	S	V	D	E	C	E	M	B	E	R	F
C	T	R	O	I	R	S	U	D	H	U	R
R	G	A	O	D	A	S	P	D	O	A	O
E	G	R	D	A	D	E	O	A	U	S	G
D	N	D	L	D	A	R	K	R	R	O	H
A	I	C	E	F	G	T	G	J	S	N	E
I	W	Y	E	M	D	Y	N	A	M	I	C
S	A	L	L	P	P	A	A	L	E	D	N
Y	R	I	A	D	I	L	S	L	V	T	A
S	D	A	N	D	E	L	I	O	N	F	D
W	I	D	H	G	E	O	N	D	U	C	K

57. DESERT

Have a look for these desert words.

CACTI GOATS PALMS
CAMELS HAZE SAHARA
DATES HEAT SANDSTORM
DESERT LIZARDS SCORPION
DUNES MIRAGE WATER
DRY OASIS

Z	O	N	E	R	K	R	E	T	A	W	E
H	A	P	P	M	I	R	A	G	E	E	R
S	T	U	A	H	C	A	C	T	I	P	D
A	E	Y	Y	L	A	C	T	I	R	G	U
N	R	Q	U	E	M	S	D	A	M	O	N
D	A	T	E	S	E	S	S	I	N	A	E
S	H	D	N	V	L	N	D	H	J	T	S
T	E	B	D	E	S	E	R	T	N	S	T
O	A	S	I	S	A	H	A	R	A	O	R
R	T	T	R	S	C	E	Z	A	H	S	I
M	R	S	C	O	R	P	I	O	N	I	S
H	A	W	T	R	I	X	L	F	I	N	G

58. BIRDS

How many birds can you spot?

CUCKOO
CROW
DUCK
FLAMINGO
JACKDAW
RAVEN

ROBIN
ROOK
SPARROW
STORK
SWALLOW
VULTURE

G	E	T	A	W	A	F	R	O	B	I	N
R	O	O	K	F	F	E	R	S	W	E	Z
A	M	T	R	O	R	S	E	T	O	K	I
V	R	E	O	E	E	R	U	T	L	U	V
E	L	Q	T	T	N	H	X	N	L	I	P
N	I	U	S	Y	K	I	E	C	A	B	M
A	N	D	J	A	C	K	D	A	W	O	T
V	S	U	Y	U	R	E	L	E	S	S	I
A	E	C	C	W	O	K	U	S	T	O	P
L	P	K	R	E	W	O	R	R	A	P	S
O	O	R	T	I	N	I	R	A	S	R	Y
O	G	N	I	M	A	L	F	L	U	P	T

59. PIZZA PICK

Pick out all the different toppings and types of pizza.

ANCHOVY
BACON
CHEESE
FROZEN
GARLIC
HAM

MOZZARELLA
OLIVES
ONIONS
PAN
PEPPERONI
PEPPERS

PINEAPPLE
SAUSAGE
SPICY
TOMATO

S	G	E	C	U	F	V	B	A	C	O	N
O	Y	V	O	H	C	N	A	C	R	R	O
G	O	O	G	L	H	A	N	T	H	E	L
A	P	E	P	P	E	R	O	N	I	M	O
R	I	C	E	D	E	A	V	E	N	M	T
L	N	U	D	G	S	X	S	F	E	E	A
I	E	A	L	L	E	R	A	Z	Z	O	M
C	A	S	N	S	X	Z	U	I	O	N	O
S	P	A	R	R	S	M	S	H	R	I	T
S	P	I	C	Y	O	R	A	S	F	O	W
O	L	I	V	E	S	G	G	H	R	N	W
P	E	P	P	E	R	S	E	T	E	S	I

60. SUMMER

Search for the summer words.

HAPPY
HEATWAVE
HOT
JUNE
JULY

MIDSUMMER
PICNIC
SAND
SEA
SUMMERTIME

SUNSHINE
SWIMMING
WARM

E	V	A	W	T	A	E	H	S	G	O	O
D	E	L	O	V	J	R	S	W	A	R	M
S	G	C	D	J	U	N	E	I	S	T	I
E	U	S	N	A	L	V	N	M	A	R	D
S	Y	N	A	R	Y	O	R	M	D	U	S
S	A	A	S	P	I	C	N	I	C	S	U
A	A	L	J	H	K	O	P	N	V	I	M
A	L	I	R	H	A	I	I	N	G	U	M
L	I	R	H	A	I	I	N	G	U	M	M
G	L	D	T	P	B	N	E	A	R	S	E
N	O	O	C	P	L	E	E	T	H	V	R
U	H	R	D	Y	Y	O	G	M	I	S	S
S	S	U	M	M	E	R	T	I	M	E	T

61. HALLOWEEN

It's Halloween! Can you find the ghostly words?

APPLES
BAT
CANDLES
COSTUME
GHOSTS
HALLOWEEN
LANTERN
MASK
OCTOBER
PARTY
PUMPKIN
WARLOCK
WITCH

```
C U P U M P K I N G S H
H C T I W H A P O H H K
A P R I E M U T S O C B
L A N T E R N O Y S A L
L I Y W N E A E Y T I U
O N P A Y T R A P S V E
W C I R C L E C R O V F
E D T L H S E L D N A C
E O B O S E A E I B S I
N L O C B S E L P P A R
M A S K D E A V A L S E
G I R L M L R H A F I M
```

62. SCARY STUFF!

Monsters, ghouls and werewolves! See if you can find them.

BEASTS
BROOMS
CREEPY
EERIE
FAIRIES
GHOULS
GOBLINS
HAUNTED
MONSTERS
SPELLS
TREATS
WEBS
WEIRD
WEREWOLF
WIZARD

```
R E W R F L O W E R E W
M O E X A L E D E F T I
O F B V I I D E C B S Z
N T S H R A G Y R C T A
S E J D I D R H G I A R
T B W S E H A U N T E D
E C K S S S G H S H R R
R R J H T X L V M A T A
S L L E P S D U O R J A
Q E A R C Y A I O K F C
Y P E E R C D E R H R O
Z X D T S N I L B O G O
```

63. SWEET TREATS

See how many things you can find in the shop.

COOKIES
CUPCAKE
ECLAIR
FLAN
GATEAU
MALLOWS
MERINGUE
MUFFINS
PASTRIES
ROLLS
SCONE

```
I S I R S N I F F U M S
E T L G H D C E J A J M
X I H L O V E L K E O I
S U A R O O Z Q I T Y R
S C O N E R R X J A C G
E O U M M E R I N G U E
I O N J A M T R F B P P
R K P R L C R I A L C E
T I A C L V A G H D A S
S E E H O A F D W G K N
A S E A W M L T E Y E D
P T A E S F E R B E U I
```

64. BAKERY

How many cakes and buns can you see?

BUNS
CAKES
CHEESECAKE
COOKIES
CRUMPETS
DOUGHNUTS
GINGERBREAD
MACAROONS
PANCAKES
PIES
SHORTBREAD
TARTS

Z	S	H	O	R	T	B	R	E	A	D	A	D	A
C	P	I	E	S	B	I	R	D	J	A	C
H	A	T	D	S	D	U	T	Y	H	E	T
M	N	T	O	P	M	I	N	U	O	R	C
A	C	R	U	M	P	E	T	S	U	B	H
C	A	I	G	L	U	U	A	E	S	R	Y
A	K	C	H	S	A	T	R	I	E	E	U
R	E	L	N	O	E	W	T	K	S	G	R
O	S	D	U	S	E	K	S	O	J	N	F
O	B	E	T	I	C	E	A	O	A	I	I
N	R	I	S	C	O	N	E	C	M	G	F
S	G	E	K	A	C	E	S	E	E	H	C

65. POST OFFICE

What can you find at the post office?

ADDRESS
CARDS
DELIVER
ENVELOPES
LETTERS
MAILBAG
MAILBOX
MESSAGE
NAMES
PACKAGE
PARCEL
STAMPS
TELEGRAMS

T	E	N	V	E	L	O	P	E	S	I	K
H	S	H	O	A	E	I	A	E	M	P	X
S	E	M	A	N	T	I	R	A	A	U	Q
A	F	M	G	H	T	I	C	A	R	D	S
D	E	L	I	V	E	R	E	D	G	S	S
W	A	R	F	L	R	B	L	B	E	T	G
S	P	M	A	T	S	E	J	R	L	E	A
T	L	O	P	I	R	N	D	E	E	D	B
H	J	E	N	B	R	D	N	N	T	O	L
O	M	E	S	S	A	G	E	B	L	E	I
R	E	G	A	K	C	A	P	I	N	K	A
F	I	F	E	V	X	O	B	L	I	A	M

66. WINTERTIME

Find the words linked to the winter season.

BLIZZARD
COLD
COZY
DECEMBER
FREEZING
FROSTY
GALES
HOLLY
ICY
RAIN
SANTA
SKATING
SKIING
SNOWMAN
STORMS
TOBOGGAN

W	I	N	S	G	N	I	Z	E	E	R	F
T	D	E	S	K	A	T	I	N	G	R	P
G	G	L	T	C	I	O	S	L	D	R	A
S	A	T	O	I	L	I	A	C	H	E	I
N	I	A	R	C	O	P	N	R	I	B	R
O	C	D	M	I	S	T	T	G	E	M	S
W	Y	T	S	O	R	F	A	S	T	E	Y
M	I	L	V	S	Z	X	Y	Z	O	C	L
A	R	S	U	E	R	E	M	I	S	E	L
N	F	G	B	L	I	Z	Z	A	R	D	O
B	E	A	U	A	T	T	R	A	E	S	H
T	O	B	O	G	G	A	N	H	H	N	I

ANSWERS

1. FISHY TAILS

```
T P Y E N C Z S Q U I D
H R O A B A L O E H T L
H A D D O C K L W F F M
V W G N I R R E H C A L
S N R L O T O M Z C L E
E S A L M O N E L V X R
S M M O V J O S K A T E
M O T B E O B L S E I K
A D A S C A M P I N S C
L R G T U R B O T S T A
Z S L E S S U M E I N M
F T S R E T S Y O R B D
```

2. DESSERT DELIGHT

```
C H E E S E C A K E J A
U N L S O T N G H P K C
S E M O L I N A G I I J
T A O B F T G H O R O O
A C U A E T A G I K F S
R S S C W C T S F L A N
D U S X O Z P O L A O L
E N E I E C E R E E G O
D D P C P K E B A V E L
Z A P P Y P I E W L P L
T E E A G E J T V M N E
F R M E R I N G U E W J
```

3. SUPERSTARS

```
S T A R L I G H T A S C
T C G C K N V V A T T E
A E T H A M A S A S A H
R N P S T A R R Y T R A
B I A T O T F Y O A F W
U H R Z I P Y O R L T
S R T T S S T A R D O M
S R Y H A R V E S U W O
T A P R O V I S T S E R
P T O P L A N S G T R N
C S T A R S H I P E D E
D A T E E Z A G R A T S
```

4. SPACE MISSION

```
A J A M P O T C O M E T
S U N A U R T I N O M E
A P E R O C K E T O D L
T I S S R P U C K N E E
S T A R B L A U T G H S
R E T B I A S O M S O C
G R U M T N H U S B N O
A B R K E E N M A R Y P
L U N E P T U N E R E E
A U R O R A S E V Y N M
X S A T U S U N A R U E
Y T U R U N I V E R S E
```

5. MAGIC WORDSEARCH

```
P K H S L L E P S H A R
H C A U L D R O N R V Y
S I L W I S H P P A Z
I R L O N E C C A M P
N T O A V B R O O M O U
A Z W S C E Y N Z T E M
V U E W W A R L O C K P
C R E T I N C L O A K
W E N S T W Z O O P A I
A B R A C A D A B R A N
N A R C H A R M R B C L
D I S A P P E A R D D E
```

6. SCHOOL IS COOL!

```
O X C C U H T A M A R W
L C A L C U L A T O R I
D O E A R A O S S R E B
E M M S A C C S V A H L
K P A S Y K S E D R C A
R U S K O O B M N E A C
O T L N A S B N A E K
W E I A S U E L B D T B
E R C H U N D Y P I O O
M A N C T R A R T N O A
O L E Y U I R A T G I R
H C P L A Y G R O U N D
```

7. WHAT'S THE BUZZ?

```
R U Z I W O E L B R A W
B U Z Z E O F F R E D O
E T R G T K C A U Q A O
L C J R A A C R I T A F
L A I E E M O O W F E V
O C P W L S K S Q F L E
W K R A B A W G R U N T
P L A P E S U N G H B T
Z E T U S N A R L E B R
Q U O I P Y T O W A J O
A S N I F F T O O H O N
C H I R P F Y Q H I S S
```

8. HAUNTED HOUSE

```
G A R G O Y L E S P I E
H A P P A M S P O O K S
S O N E Y L I H P T O N
P S E R I P M A V S S M
E A Y R N T W N O S C O
C A L G H O S T S S A N
T T I H L Q W O E E R S
E C K O R O E M E I V
R C E U O Q A S H B E E
S K M L W U L L K M C R
F T U S K E L E T O N S
F L O W E R E W A Z H P
```

9. TREASURE CHEST

```
D A Z Z A M E T H Y S T
R R Z A E K E G A N D U
U D I A M O N D S T O R
B R R P E L O N S N T O
Y W C K R E B M A A Q U
B C O C A S C O P D P O
A H N Z L G T L P N A I
N L O G D J N C H E Z S
G A V V S H E T P A E
L R T E L E C A R B A T
E O A J M I N T E D A J
E C A L K C E N A C G O
```

10. FAB FRUIT

```
C R O O R A N G E Y E S
H A B A N A N A A T L T
E S N O O R Y P N Q P R
R E J O V A R B W Q P A
R S T P L U M O T T A W
Y R R E B E S O O G E
S H R A N O M E L D N E
C A G R A P E S O F I R
T W I K I R I W I R P R
F A T R A S P B E R R Y
T O C I R P A A R H A Y
D P E A C H S E T A D O
```

11. COLOR CRAZY

```
F R O L L A V I N R A C
I J E E S W O B N I A R
R A M C S C R F T E D A
E B A Q D G E M S S E Y
W M R U C A T H U H H O
O T B A L L O O N S T N
R O L E O J R G R O O S
K M E R W T R C I T H O
S A S E N H A H S U O M
R S T N I A R I E P O C
I F W H H F W L N E O N
T E S N U S F R U I T S
```

12. CANDY STORE

```
C A N D Y B R L Y T L S
A E T T E B R E H S O L
R I U Q C E K I T S L I
A S G U M D R O P S L C
M X R T I A R T W O O
E F T F N S E H N C P R
L G O S T H C C S S O I
S V F I S M M S S V P C
I X F R S N B B W O S
E J E G D U F O S E Z E
G U E E T A L O C O H C
M A R S H M A L L O W G
```

13. FLOWER GARDEN

```
M A R I G O L D B O R O
D C A L B A E D L R O J
V B U T T E R C U P S K
A R V T H A S T E T E S
E O Q D S T W E B I V U
P O C A L I L V E M T C
T G W I A R R E L B S O
E F Y S N A P U L E E R
E R P Y G O O O E I C C
W O P Z O I N M A V L E
S N O W D R O P M I L Y
T M P K C O H Y L L O H
```

14. TREEHOUSE

```
T R H S R I B I S C K S
E E C H E S T N U T A T
H U H W C D C A P U R S
B O E T G P A L M K T E
I T S R S R A T W M E R
U E R R A L P O P O O O
N B Y L U H I W I H K M
L E Q U K R S A S T E A
A F I Z A A E N H M I C
W I L L O W C R H U I Y
A R L A R O Z O O L A S
A P P L E B R A E P I E
```

15. SEASHORE SEARCH

```
O S E L T S A C D N A S
S T T S W I U G A V E E
C A H U C R D A V D W A
W R E R W A V E S R S W
O F S F C R E P S U P E
T I R O C K P O O L P E
V S H O L I D O S C I D
I H I S H D T A O B S X
K F P S L K S K Y A I U
O S W I M M E R S R E T
S H E L L S F I V C S P
M A J H S I F Y L L E J
```

16. WILD WEATHER

```
H U R R I C A N E R R F
A C Y C L O N E R D T R
I S O W O R D C A S S E
L T R O R I B C V E E E
S N O W L Y B M N W R Z
T O R N A D O B C E E E
O S D E J N U H O T D N
R D B R O I H A P E N G
M B C V F W P Z I O U Z
M Y D U O L C Y W I H S
I C A C G L F R O S T S
L I G H T N I N G O G G
```

17. FUNNY WORDS

```
S N I G G E R H G A G C
W A V E R C C A Y K I T
E W K A L A T O K E S E
L A U G H T E P T U U M
T I W I V B S Z L W O H
R C W G B O T Q M K R Y
A L Y G I C A R T O O N
H E N L J X D O Y R M U
C O M E D Y J J E A U P
A V L O Z Y N N U F H M
B R I D A Y L R O R F N
Y S U O I R A L I H J O
```

18. ANIMALS

```
S T S C C G H E O O P V
T A H D O G S Y T T L A
I R E I W R A E S R O H
B V E T H D E K O P C A
B E P I G I R N U I N M
A V C A M O T O A R V S
R R E A X S T D F C A T
E Y S N E K C I H C S E
S S K C U D H S R O U R
O Z E H F S B M A L A M
M I C E I L A T T E Y P
P R O G G O A T S N Q M
```

19. TOYS!

```
O T A O B O O C K I B E
O R R I K N B F E E B T
R A T T L E H O U Z I T
Q U V S N O Y A R C M
S N O W B R I O X X Y O
R I A D O L L Y M K C O
S O W O N L H O P C L N
K H E I M A U W A A E B
A I O T A B S B I L B O
T M C G B A I T N T H N
E B O A P R V E T I K N
S E M A G A Z Y S K N E
```

20. GROCERY STORE

```
I T W C O O K I E S S S
E C F F O C H T K L I M
E A V I E R S W S E R A
N C G H A E U S U G A R
M S T R P P M Z I G T M
S A E E M P S Y U S I A
C D J C H E E S E X O L
S C R D H P G C A S L A
O E M A R G A R I N E D
U C R E T T U B T A G E
P Z E R G W H J L E O O
T A V B H N O C A B B A
```

21. VEGETABLE PATCH

```
J E Z U C C H I N I V E
O E R T S Q U A S H I R
F S S K A L E F R E D E
E T L O C C O R B O E W
S S E D E A U O A L N O
E P G A A R W N O D J
O T A B U R N P C E F
I N B E L O Z O O E Q I
A A B E T T K N K B X L
T C A T F F J S F B S U
O H C E K O H C I T R A
P A S T U O R P S Z X C
```

22. OCEANS AND SEAS

```
D E R A H O U B L A C K
R E F B I A T E R R T G
E C A S P I A N O C H P
F I T C P P U F W T I A
C D J I V G L I P C
I A E K E W A K C N I
T A N T A R C T I C A F
A B T F L Q X G D M I
D K M R Y I A A D C
R E C A R I B B E A N L
D V U G N S Z J D W I N
A T H T R O N K T I M O
```

23. WHAT'S IN THE BATHROOM?

```
T H I M B L V K N I S U
O S E L I T E W S T P Q
P U R R S H A M P O O H
H R Q U H S A U R I N T
O B W S O A P T S L G A
R H W R W A N T I E E B
D T O W E L C H I T G E
E O E D R L H A F U O L
N O F A U C E T G H I B
T O O T H P A S T E B
A C A T Y H O T F A U U
M I R R O R F A T B O B
```

24. WHAT'S IN THE KITCHEN?

```
R O L P D O T R I F E C
E V S T O V E E B R I I
F E K P K E E D E E A N
R P C I O N S N L E L K
I I W J S E R E A Z H A
G N P G R I L L C E O Y
E C O J P U T B K R B L
R E T S A O T O P P U S
A C S S N O T H A T I
T V A R S S G E H E R N
O X I I P E E L T T E K
R Z E V A W O R C I M K
```

25. BIRDS

```
A C T I C B U N S X Z N
P A R R O T Q R E N V I
R N A T W L A P W I N G
D A R E I B E E F O G H
R R C N B N T X W I N T
Y H N C O E W D I R I
B A A I R M P I G E O N
K R A I J A N T A R T G
C W O P S G O G H R S A
A C A T X P W B L O R L
L A T H W N A D O V E
B U D G I E E W N W F R
```

26. GO NUTS!

```
G R M A H C A S H E W
N X A L L R T R E U A
B A C O R N L B F U E L
A E A G O F I O I R G N
S D Z H A Z E L I G U
E E A E A H A I B T R T
A L M O N D R P E U D S
N I I T S T B H R N H W
U A A B F S D P T O J R
N T U N T S E H C K H
G P I S T A C H I O S D
T U N D N U O R G C W R
```

27. PRIVATE DETECTIVE

```
T R F A C T S E E V J K
O T C R I M E E S T V M
Y S L E U T H N A V A U
I L U J E V J K M R I T
C E E V E J I G Y T C Y
I M S E O N E U T N U H
S J F O O R P O I Z A C
N A O H L Q A R T R A I
E C I S K Y T E N S O R
R C G M D D E T E T Y I
O A R U Y A T A D J A C
F I N G E R P R I N T S
```

28. ROBOTS

```
S H I S L O R T N O C S
P T E C H N O L O G Y S
D V N O U F B H E R B E
V N I M H G O H O R O C
H K H P S D T M A X R O
U W C U E C E B A R G R
M S A T D M A R G O R P
A X M E C I T E R E U E
N I D R B J U N E I E J
O E C I T S I R U T U F
N T E L L I G E N C E
D I O R D N A S T E R Z
```

29. AROUND THE WORLD

```
S P A I N Y I N A P A J
W K I C O M M M J F M R
E E S E S O U S X E E D
D C S L P N A T I R B
E D U A L O G H P W U
N S R N A R L O Y A C Z
E C M D V W E U G C A E
C H O A C A B S E I S
N I T A L Y E E V R R C
A N D R H I T R E F R I
R A U S T R A L I A I C
F R O I L Y N A M R E G
```

30. GLOBE TROTTERS

```
I A V A L L C A N A D A A
N H M E X I C O F I N U
D U Y O R Z N R O B A S
I N E K R A M N E D L T
A G K G R R E A T N R R
X A R E X B W D H A E
E R U T D F E Z A Z A
C Y T R U E T E N T R
E P O R T U G A L V
E Q E R C V G H A F W A
R R C H O L L A N D S L
G R E E N L A N D J R O
```

31. CREEPY-CRAWLY

```
B I R F S L U G A L O R
C E G R E A C U T Y O A
O K E X D G U B Y D A L
C A A T I Q U O T R S L
K K R R L M R O W I C
R D W A E E W L E F G P
O O J S P I D E R B R
A K G A P T O V V W X E
C A Y P A R A S I T E T
H I T A R A N T U L A R A
A H E D E P I T N E C
J N O I P R O C S Z O I
```

32. INCREDIBLE INSECTS!

```
F I R E F L Y T H O C E
L P R I B C Z W T A N G
E S H O R N E T R E P D
A S T I R S H J J L O
I I G M O O C W C I T N M
T R D O P A R K V T M A
P E D O T I U Q S O M R
T E P Z O H I V S B V T
P I S S I G M T O E T O
T F A H A R L O C U S T
X L W A F R E R S L U S
I Y L F R E T T U B U H
```

33. GOBBLEDYGOOK

```
Z A H P P Y L L I S Y O
A N S A B R A B U H R O
G O B B L E D Y G O O K
M N O W T B L A G H T F
M S C A R T E B F S L B
A E H F A B L E M A L
L N A F L E T B I U N E
F S F L E S T E T P C T
M E Q V A A L U E H
A U N N R G L D T E
L Z I G R R P I B D U R
F L A P D O O D L E I R
```

34. MUSICAL INSTRUMENTS

```
B R I P J U S O O Z A K
A G U I T A R S R I E E
C T N A A R U O E P N Y
I E R N W T L I D M I B
N I L O I V E L R W R O
O R A I T I S R O Q U A
M B A N J O O L C U O R
R E Q D F L U T E O B D
A L R E F A Y R R I M R
H L U T E I T G N S A A
L S V E S H O P I E T T
O S C S E P I P G A B H
```

35. "A" WORDS

```
A S T R O N A U T G O R
S P R V E A T D R C J N
T A Q U A M A R I N E C
R P A T A B O R C A E E
O R A C U E A W T K L D
N I A R C R T C S J O S
O I L O P A A Z U R E A
M R A N A L B A G S R L
Y O D I D O S O U O S A
F W D N O Z A M A L V S
D L S C I T R O L W K
M M N B B S A L T A Q A
```

36. MORE "A" WORDS

```
H E R E H P S O M T A U
A M I L K I R O S E R H
D N O M L A A R C T C
V B E W A A P P L E T O
E U A S T E R O I D H U
N Z N T M C T T A M S
T Z E I A R C A D E E R
U R S T P K O H A W T C
R A N E R A T K I T Z
E S E I O N N O I T C A
A T O M N R U B U A S Q
A L P H A B E T K A J U
```

37. BIRTHDAYS!

```
S R I B O G I F T S S N S
I C I N G O R D E N U F
N W H I T E B L A C K
C N I C N A D T R I P S
I S C E L E B R A T E H
N H A P P Y C H D A R O
G E K S T N E S E R P R
M E E R Y A W O R O L P
U S T A N D R A S C L A
S L A R T S G A M E S R
C R O F R I E N D S
C A N D L E S W F G H Y
```

38. DOGS

```
R E L G A E D D B P W Y
O G J A L S A T I O N O
T N S O S S X H M W A
T E A M V H S C T E O B
W E M H H E E A M R L E
E R R I E E T S I A F S
I S E S R P O J H N H E
L A B R A D O R T I O N
E Z O L G O R M T A U
R D D R I C R O C N N K
A R D N U H S H C A D E
A S E T T E R H A P I P
```

41. SOCCER CRAZY

```
R S T B S L C O R N E R
I M K E T U H U E D S E
T L C W E V Z O F O U L
L M K I N E N E E R B E
I R L H T M W A R D S G
K A E I I A A R E B T A
E T F K N N S H E O I T
E D T O S A E J T R T I
Y F F L A G C I K A U O
A E A R E E R O C S T N
S O C C E R B K N E A
G E K N R A S E K E Y F
```

39. MORE DOGS

```
A D O G I L E I N A P S
C A I R E D A L E I O T
D L E E A D E R S T O B
N M A V C R O I L C D L
U A U B O X E R A H L O
O T B U L L D O G I E O
H I K L S C U E H I D
Y A W H P R E T U U H
E N C O E T E A C A L O
R M P U T Y K S U H A U
G E R B I E F O P U C N
N E W F O U N D L A N D
```

40. TRAIN STATION

```
B S E G A I R R A C H W
R E A D S T E K C I T H
S D R I V E R I V A I I
R E E A W I F E A L M S
E A P S I G N A L S E T
F V E E I L D R O J I
F I E S T B S D E P A E
U P L A T F O R M D B P
B D S U N N E A W S P
A S U R E T N U H S E A
W O R G H O R G S Q U I
T A S R E G N E S S A P
```

42. COWBOY RANCH

```
R E G N A R D R H A W R
A S C A R F B R O N C O
R T R U E B E X R I O U
S E I R I A R P S E V J
T R O U G H V E E A C B
E E C A T T L E L G F E
T W O D B A V H O U S A
S E W I X O B S R E S H
O I B S V R L S P A H E
N E O A E V U P A R K N
S D Y D S L A R I A T A
J O J E L D D A S W O R
```

43. CIRCUS

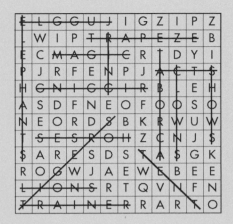

```
E L G G U J I G Z I P Z
L W I P T R A P E Z E B
E C M A G E R I D Y I
P J R F E N P J A C T S
H G N I C C I R B L E H
A S D F N E O F O O S O
N E O R D S B K R W U W
T S E S R O H Z C N J S
S A R E S D S T A S G K
R O G W J A E W E B E E
L I O N S R T Q V N F N
T R A I N E R R A R T O
```

44. COMPUTERS

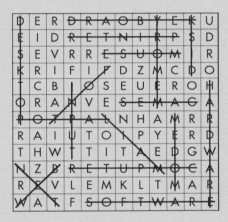

```
D E R D R A O B Y E K U
E I D R E T N I R P S D
S E V R R E S U O M R
K R I F I P D Z M C D O
T C B O S E U E R O H
O R A N V E S E M A G A
P O T P A L N H A M R R
R A I U T O I P Y E R D
T H W T T I T A E D G W
N Z B R E T U P M O C A
R X V L E M K L T M A R
W A T F S O F T W A R E
```

45. STAR SIGNS

```
S C O R P I O T Y A M D
A S A R D N W A R I E S
G O A T A W U A Y Q V
I E S E N M R R M T E N
T A V S L E P U H I L E
T A R F E G E S C L T P
A R B L G R P A T E O
R E A S C O H U T G
B R H W I J S D B O R
U U C A P R I C O R N
S Q U E R T E E Z I S V
A Q U A R I U S H I P Y
```

46. HERBS

```
S E T A F A E L Y A B L
A M A R J O R A M C A R
L Y S P E P O R C S O
R H S A T M A N N H I S
E T K I G M I X T E L E
D O F E X E E M J R K M
N R L E N N E F D V D A
A J L O E V A Z A T R
I C I Q Z P A R S L E Y
R E D R L I F T E X E R
O S T S A V O R Y O U W
C H I V E S O N D A R O
```

47. CHRISTMAS

```
S D R A C B S U V K A Y
V E A T R R E A K F A S
M C H R I S T M A S D S
I E Q E C E B D E R Y T
S M Y E R S C A R O L S
T B J T I M H N T A T D
L E K N H G E L S N N
E R K A S R M A E S M A
I L E P H N P S R W L
O U Y N D F E V N F A R
E L H O L L Y D Y I A
E D H S T D B S T F I G
```

48. FESTIVE FUN

```
R U D O L P H F A I R Y
E A R T C H J K E S W U
I F A V R T S T H G I
N E V E Y J T S Z S H E
D S E L B U A B A T T
E C R S I S R T N U A
E H T F E A S T A N S D
R A T M E L E M O T N E
W T I F W M D S A S H U
O N C O L D B N M E F D
R A N F A D R D A H J K
K S N O I T A R O C E D
```

49. FIRE STATION

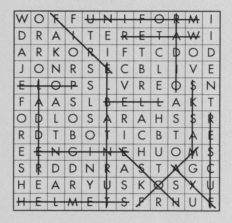

```
W O F F U N I F O R M I
D R A I T E R E T A W I
A R K O R I F T C D O D
J O N R S E C B L I V E
E L O P S L V R E O S N
F A A S L B E L L A K T
O D L O S A R A H S S R
R D T B O T I C B T A E
E E N G I N E H U O M S
S R D D N R A S T X G C
H E A R Y U S K O S X U
H E L M E T S P R N U E
```

50. "B" WORDS

```
F B H B I B M B L B T A
B I N O C U L A R S A C
L E N B T M N I M O T
O L Y F L D A E R Y
S I I U E O N L A J S
S O H R E R R A U J K A
O N E E B I N B O Y F
M S E V E X L U O R T K
R S B K L E A J B F U A
X A O G I C K G U I A E
B O B A M B O O Z L E R
B U B B L E V R Z S B B
```

51. PUZZLE WORDS

```
W A I C R Y P T I C R O
O K E J C R U Z O O C E
R Y N A R A Z A Q U I Z
D N I M E B Z X G D G A
S R G R W A L C L U O M
E R A M Y S T E R Y F I A
A A A N E J G S A W
R H Z D A I E D O C K O
C R B R I V E D L L S O
H P O T B R W L D U D F
Q U E O M I G E W E R I
A S N O I T U L O S O H
```

52. COOL!

```
I C H I L L Y D D V W
R R B A L K R G J Y C
I A S N O W F L A K E N
R L N I U N R L R O L T
C O O E C O O L C A A R
S P W V O Y S U T I N Y
T E S I J T R I O D E
E D T H D N B I C T L L
E N O T S L A H V E A
L J R N I O T R H X S E
S T M I O R E I C A L G
B R U E G N I Z E E R F
```

53. IT'S A JUNGLE!

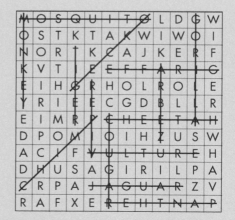

```
M O S Q U I T O L D G W
O S T K T A K W I W O I
N O R T K C A J K E R F
K V T I E F F A R I G
E I H G R H O L R O L E
Y R I E E C G D B L L R
E I M R Y C H E E T A H
D P O M I O I H Z U S W
A C I F V U L T U R E H
D H U S A G I R I L P A
Q R P A J A G U A R Z V
R A F X E R E H T N A P
```

54. JUNGLE FUN!

```
S A N D S R U C O B R A
P I R A N H A R D A X X
I A R V A E D O N I H R
D G H H K J T C S H L O
E O A M E D B O P P H H
R R N O O Y J D I F O R
I B T N G I E I I O N O
A N E Y H L S I D C Z S
S F L J L R E E M E D E
L E O P A R D R D O L L S
E M P E N I C N W O L I
M A E L E P H A N T I G
```

57. DESERT

```
Z O N E R K R E T A W E
H A R P M I R A G E E R
S T U A H C A C T I P D
A E Y Y L A C T I R G U
N R Q U E M S D A M O N
B A T E S E S S I N A E
S H D N V L N D H J T S
T E B D E S E R T N S T
O A S I S A H A R A O R
R T T R S C E Z A H S I
M R S C O R P I O N I S
H A W T R I X I F I N G
```

55. "C" WORDS

```
S A F E T A L O C O H C
I N C I N D E R E L L A
A C A A H O U S E E R L
V S P O R C I N E M A C
T A E T T A K T A C U
N T V O A H Q E S R E L
R J A T C M M O A A V A
A N N E H O S R N C A T
C A N D L R U A Q C O
D Y R R E H C U P H Q R
C C A L E N D A R R C S
D T E F A C S T O T Y F
```

56. "D" WORDS

```
S E L Z Z A D F R E S I
E S V D E C E M B E R F
C T R O I R S U D H U R
R G A O D A S P D O A O
E G R D A D E O A U S G
D N D L D A R K R R O H
A I C E F G T G J S N E
W Y E M D Y N A M I C
S A L L P P A A L E D N
Y R A D I L S L V T A
S D A N D E L I O N F D
W I D H G E O N D U C K
```

58. BIRDS

```
G E T A W A F R O B I N
R O O K F F E R S W E Z
A M T R O R S E T O K I
V R E O E E R U T L U V
E L Q T T N H X N L I P
N I U S Y K I E C A B M
A N D J A C K D A W O T
V S U Y U R E L E S S I
A E C C W O K U S T O P
L P K R E W O R R A P S
O O R T I N I R A S R Y
O G N I M A L F L U P T
```

59. PIZZA PICK

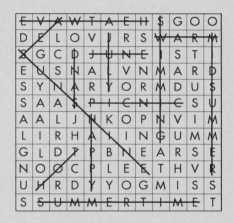

```
S G E C U F V B A C O N
O Y V O H C N A C R R O
G O O G L H A N T H E L
A P E P P E R O N I M O
R I C E D E A V E N M T
L N U D G S X S F E E A
I E A L L E R A Z Z O M
C A S M S X Z U I O N O
S P A R R S M S H R I T
S P I C Y O R A S F O W
O L I V E S G G H R N W
P E P P E R S E T E S I
```

60. SUMMER

```
E V A W T A E H S G O O
D E L O V I R S W A R M
X G C D J U N E I S T
E U S N A L V N M A R D
S Y N A R Y O R M D U S
A A S P I C N I C S U
A A L J H K O P N V I M
L I R H A I N G U M M
G L D Z P B N E A R S E
N O O C P L E E T H V R
U H R D Y Y O G M I S S
S S U M M E R T I M E T
```

61. HALLOWEEN

```
C U P U M P K I N G S H
H C T I W H A P O H H K
A P R I E M U T S O C B
L A N T E R N O Y S A L
L I Y W N E A E Y Z I U
O N P A Y T R A P S V E
W C I R C L E C R O V F
E D T L H S E L D N A C
E O B O S E A E I B S I
N L O C B S E L P P A R
M A S K D E A V A L S E
G I R L M L R H A F I M
```

62. SCARY STUFF!

```
R E W R F L O W E R E W
M O E X A L E D E F T I
O F B V I D E C B S Z I
N T S H R A G Y R C T A
S E J D D R H G I A R R
T B W S E H A U N T E D
E C K S S S G H S H R R
R R J H T X L V M A T A
S L L E P S D U O R J A
Q E A R C Y A I O K F C
Y P E E R C D E R H R O
Z X D T S N I L L O G O
```

64. BAKERY

```
Z S H O R T B R E A D A
C P I E S B I R D J A C
H A T D S D U T Y H E T
M N T O P M I N U O R C
A C R U M P E T S U B H
C A I G L U U A E S R Y
A K C H S A T R E E U
R E L N O E W T K S G R
O S D U S E K S O J N F
O B E T I C E A O A I I
N R I S C O N E G M G F
S G E K A C E S E E H C
```

63. SWEET TREATS

```
I S I R S N I F F U M S
E T L G H D C E J A J M
X I H L O V E L K E O I
S U A R O O Z Q I T Y R
S C O N E R R X J A C G
E Q U M M E R I N G U E
I O N J A M T R F B P P
R K P R L C R I A L C E
T I A C L V I G H D A S
S E E H O A F D W G K N
A S E A W M L T E Y E D
P T A E S F E R B E U I
```

65. POST OFFICE

```
T E N V E L O P E S I K
H S H O A E I A E M P X
S E M A N T I R A A U Q
A F M G H T I C A R D S
D E L I V E R E D G S S
W A R F L R B I B E T G
S P M A T S E J R L E A
T L O P I R N D E E D B
H J E N B R D N N T O L
O M E S S A G E B L E
R E G A K C A P I N K A
F I F E V X O B L I A M
```

66. WINTERTIME

```
W I N S G N I Z E E R F
T D E S K A T I N G R P
G G L T C I O S L D R A
S A T O I L I A C H E I
N I A R C O P N R I B R
O C D M I S T T G E M S
W Y T S O R F A S T E Y
M I L V S Z X Y Z O C L
A R S U E R E M I S E L
N F G B L I Z Z A R D O
B E A U A T T R A E S H
T O B O G G A N H H N I
```

Picture Puzzles

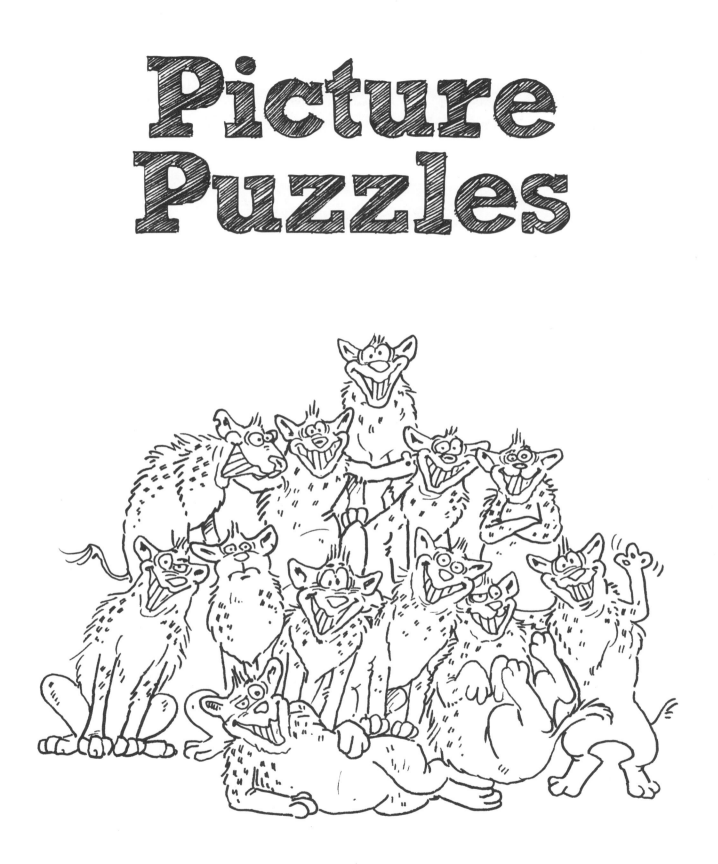

1. Freaky Footprints

Which monster left this footprint?

1. 2. 3. 4. 5.

2. Mumbo Jumbo

Spot the difference between the six elephants. Who is the odd one out?

1. 2. 3. 4. 5. 6.

3. Shadow Bats

Which shadow matches the vampire bat?

1. 2. 3. 4. 5.

4. Crossroads

You're lost! Study the clues to find which road to take.

Clues

1. Avoid hens, cows and sheep.
2. Don't go North.
3. Head for the hills.
4. Go the opposite way from the wood.

5. Speedboat

Which skier is attached to the speedboat?

6. Jaws

Which shark took a bite out of the raft?

7. Haunted House

Circle the ten spooks hiding in the haunted house.

8. Mystery Tour

Which route should the mystery tour bus take to get out of the maze?

MYSTERY TOUR

9. Spider's Web

Which spider's web trail leads to the center of the web?

1.

2.

10. Snakes Alive
Which snake has a rattle on the end of its tail?

11. Silly Sheep
How many sheep are there in the picture?

12. Spot the Difference
Spot the dog has lost seven spots. Circle where they are missing.

13. Bungee Monkey

Which monkey has the longest bungee cord?

14. Mosquito Match

Two of these mosquitoes match. Which two are identical?

15. Goo Who?

Who is covered in goo?

16. Alien Eyeballs

How many eyeballs does the alien have? Follow the eyeball trails to see which ones are connected to its head.

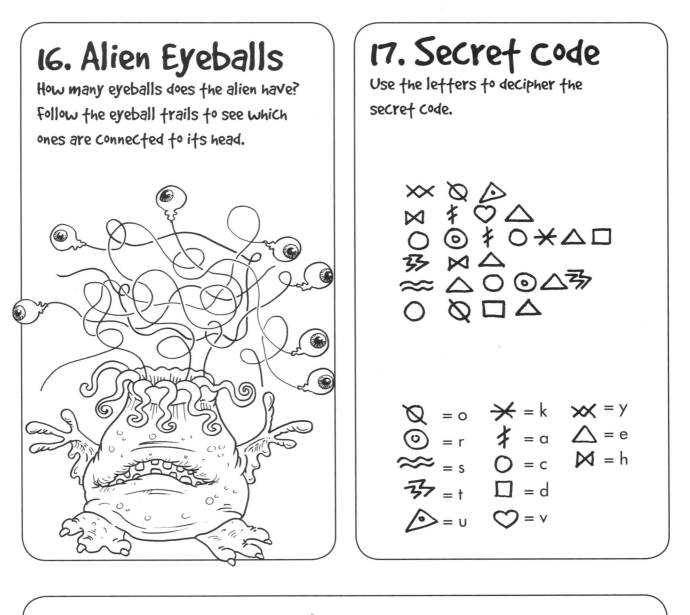

17. Secret Code

Use the letters to decipher the secret code.

⊘	=	o
⊙	=	r
≈	=	s
⌁	=	t
△ (u)	=	u
✳	=	k
⌁ (a)	=	a
○	=	c
□	=	d
♡	=	v
⋈	=	y
△	=	e
⋈ (h)	=	h

18. Snowbody There

oh yes there is! Five polar bears are hiding in the snowscene. Can you find them?

19. Cat Splat

Which splat mark did the crazy cat make?

1.   2.   3.

4.   5.   6.

20. Witches' Hats

Draw three straight lines across the box to leave three different witches' hats in each part.

21. Top Secret

Use the secret code to read the message on the computer.

⊀ = a
@ = s
✓ = d
✶ = e
▽ = g
Ⅱ = h
⊠ = i

♡ = m
▢ = o
≈ = r
◎ = c
⊘ = t
▽ = u
= w

22. Mummy Mummy!

Can you spot the two identical mummies?

1.

2.

3.

4.

5.

6.

23. Bubble Trouble

Oops! Someone has used too much bubble bath.
Who is it?

1.

2.

3.

4.

5.

24. Laughing Hyenas

How many hyenas are smiling in
the picture?

25. Blackout!

How many animals are hiding in the dark?

26. Howl at the Moon

Can you spot the two pictures that are identical?

1.
2.
3.
4.
5.
6.

27. Bugs!

Draw along the dotted lines to form five equal-sized portions. Each portion should contain only one of each bug.

28. Mad Mars

Is there life on Mars? How many Martians can you see?

29. Wizard!

Can you help the wizard find his way out of the maze?

30. Crazy Castle

Which road leads to the crazy castle?

31. Computer Connection

Which game controller is connected to the computer?

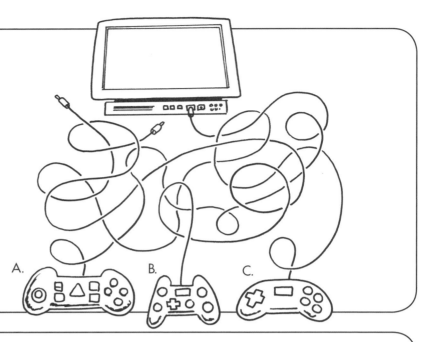

A. B. C.

32. Nine Dots

Use a pencil to join all nine dots without lifting your pencil off the page and without going back on any lines you've made. You can only draw four lines.

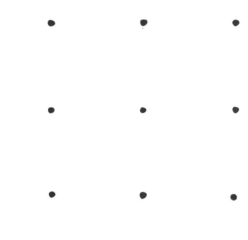

33. Over the Waves

Shade in all the shapes marked with a dot to find the shape hidden in the picture.

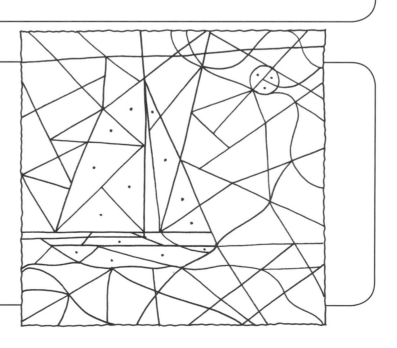

34. Under the Sea

Shade in all the shapes marked with a dot to find the shape hidden in the picture.

35. River Rapids

Which river rapid will take you safely to the lagoon?

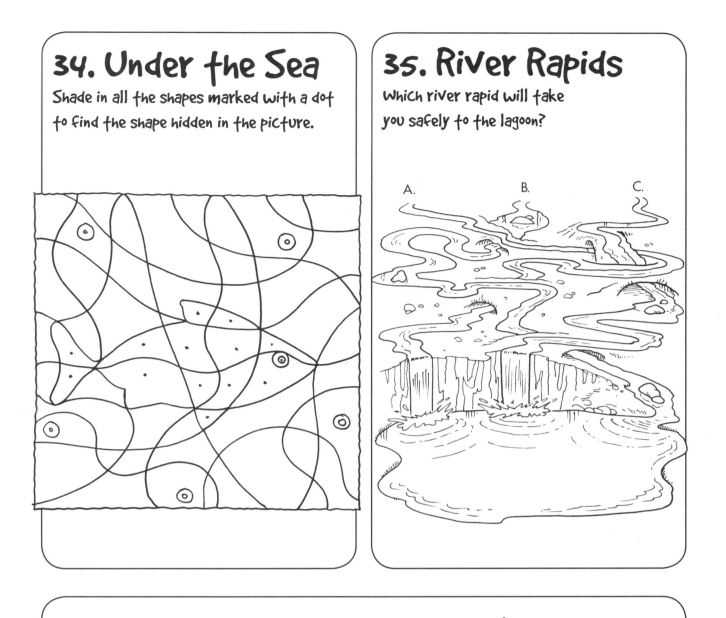

A. B. C.

36. Sailing Boat

Without lifting your pencil off the page, start at the big dot and join the dots to make a sailing boat.

37. Clown Shapes

How many circles, triangles and squares can you see in the picture of the clown?

38. Envelope

Join the dots without lifting your pencil off the paper (and without going back over any lines) to draw an envelope.

39. Manic Monkeys

How many monkeys are there in the picture?

40. Space Rocket

Two of these rockets are the same. Can you spot them?

1.
2.
3.
4.
5.
6.

41. Robot Shapes

How many circles, rectangles, triangles and squares make up the robot?

42. Sweet Boxes

Which two sweets are in every box?

43. Shadow Match

Draw lines to join each item to its matching shadow.

44. Strawberry Patch

How many strawberries are there in the strawberry patch?

45. Dog and Bone

This dog has lost his bone. Can you help him find it?

46. Teddy's Bedroom
Spot the ten differences in the picture. circle them with a pencil.

47. Snowman
Which snowman is the odd one out?

1.
2.
3.
4.
5.
6.

48. Cake Puzzle
Draw two straight lines across the box to leave three different cakes in each part.

49. Flight of Fright

Shade in all the shapes marked with a dot to find the shape hidden in the picture.

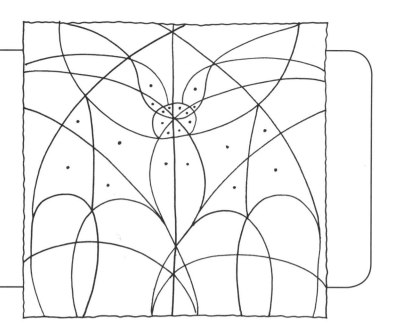

50. Fit for a King

Shade in all the shapes marked with a dot to find the shape hidden in the picture.

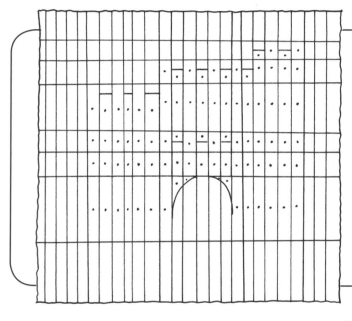

51. Top Secret

Follow the lines to find the key that opens the top secret file.

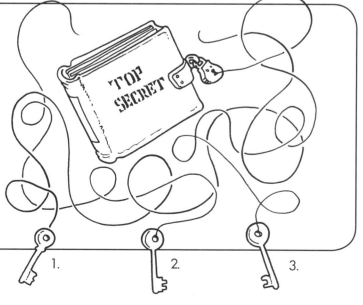

1.   2.   3.

52. Treasure Trail

Which route leads to the treasure trove?

53. Splish Splat!

Two of these splish splats are identical. Can you spot them?

1.
2.
3.
4.
5.
6.

54. Smiling Faces

Draw three straight lines (which can cross each other) to divide the circle into six parts. Each part must contain three different faces.

55. High-Five Spider

Can you spot the ten differences between these two pictures?

56. Bats' Castle

How many bats are hiding in and around the castle?

57. Star Gazing

How many stars can you see in the picture?

58. Alien Adventure

Which route should the alien spaceship take to reach its home planet?

59. Blast Off

Shade in all the shapes marked with a dot to find the shape hidden in the picture.

60. Kick It

Shade in all the shapes marked with a dot to find the shape hidden in the picture.

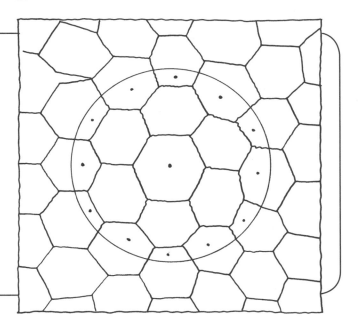

61. Cat Calling

Who is the cat phoning? Follow the lines to find out if it is the duck, the gerbil or the dog.

62. Oodles of Doodles

Two of these doodles are identical. Which two?

1.
2.
3.
4.
5.
6.

63. Jungle Trap

You are trapped in the jungle. Can you find your way out?

START

64. Sun, Moon and Stars

Draw three straight lines (which can cross each other) to divide the box into five parts. Each part must contain one sun, one moon and one star.

65. Zippy the Snail

Zippy is in a hurry to get out of the snail maze. Which route is the fastest?

66. Cat Nap

How many cats are napping in this picture?

67. Wibbly Wobbly

Two of these wibbly wobbly men are identical. Can you spot them?

1.

2.

3.

4

5.

6.

68. Walkies

Shade in the shapes marked with a dot to find the shape hidden in the picture.

69. Home Sweet Home

Shade in all the shapes marked with a dot to find the shape hidden in the picture.

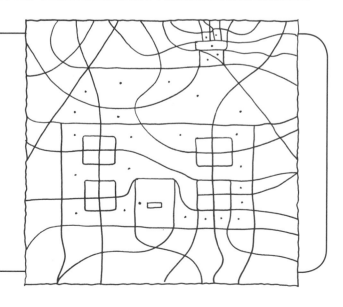

70. Shadow Shark
Which shadow belongs to the shark?

71. Beware of the Werewolf
Which shadow matches the werewolf?

72. Splatman
Which shadow matches Splatman?

73. Maze Race

Quick! How do you get out of the maze?

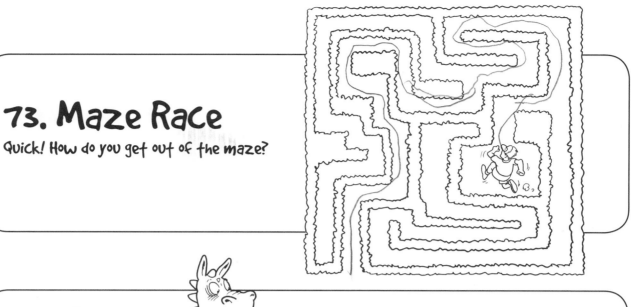

74. Sneaky Sandwich

Who took a sneaky bite out of the sea monster's sandwich? Follow the crumb trails to find out.

A.   B.   C.

75. Shadow Match

Draw a line to join each item to its matching shadow.

76. Fast Fly
What's the quickest route for the fly to take to reach the flowers?

77. Growly Grizzly
Which growly grizzly silhouette matches the real one?

78. Oops!
There are ten differences between these pictures. Can you spot them?

79. Farm Fun

How many animals can you see in the picture?

80. Wrong Way

One creature in every row is pointing in the opposite direction. Circle the odd one out in each row.

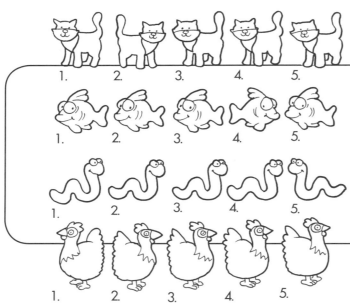

1. 2. 3. 4. 5.

1. 2. 3. 4. 5.

1. 2. 3. 4. 5.

1. 2. 3. 4. 5.

81. Teddy Bears

How many teddy bears are there in this picture?

82. Snowflakes

Two of these snowflake pictures match. Which two?

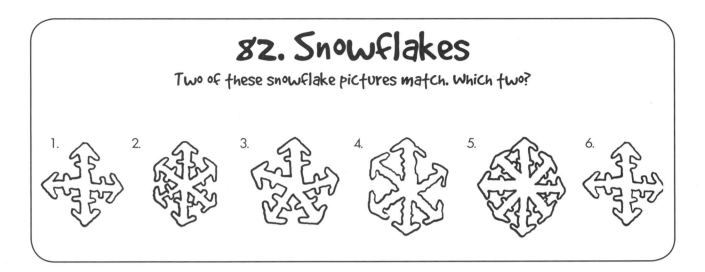

1. 2. 3. 4. 5. 6.

83. Fruity Split

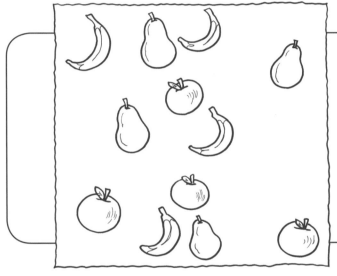

Draw two straight lines (which can cross each other) to divide the box into four parts. Each part must contain one banana, one apple and one pear.

84. Squeaky Floorboards

Shh! Keep quiet! What is the only way to get out of the maze without stepping on the squeaky floorboards?

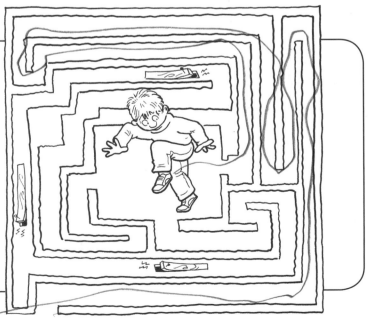

85. Vulture Trouble

Which vulture is the odd one out?

1. 2. 3.

4. 5. 6.

86. Kitty Tree

How many cats are hiding up and around the tree?

87. Ancient Book

What is the secret message written in the book? Use the letter code to find out.

□ = a   ◎ = p
∿ = b   ♡ = r
△ = e   ▨ = s
Ϝ = g   ○ = t
▽ = k   ✚ = u
Ϟ = l   ✱ = z
◊ = o

88. Busy Bees

Draw lines to join each pair of bees.

89. Squid's Hid

Shade in the parts that have a dot to reveal the hidden image.

90. Rocket Science

Which cord leads to the space rocket?

91. Bathtime Tiger

There are ten differences between these two pictures. Can you spot them?

92. Private Detective

Which trail leads to the secret footprints?

93. Find the Fairies

Seven little fairies are hiding in the woods. Can you find them?

94. Lion Match

Two of these lions are the same. Which two?

95. Gift Box

Draw three straight lines across the box to divide it into four parts. Each part must contain three different presents.

96. Zany Zebras

How many zebras are there in the picture?

97. Duck!

Which pond contains the most ducks?

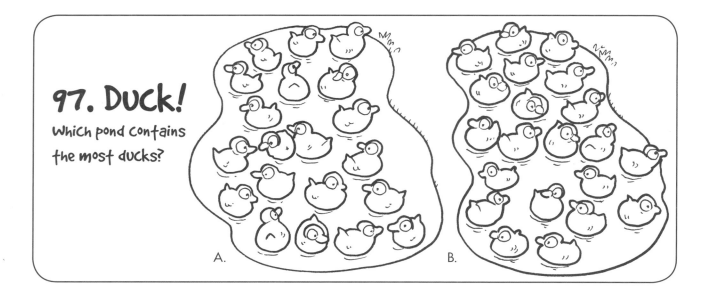

A.

B.

98. Lovely Leaves

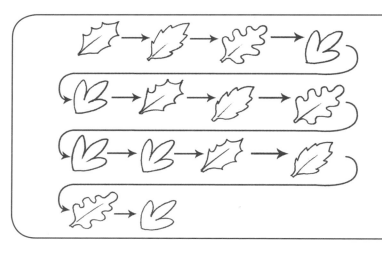

Follow the leaf trail and look at the leaf pattern. Which leaf comes next?

99. Secret Agent

Can you help the secret agent out of the maze?

100. Which Witch?

Which witch does this shadow belong to?

101. Halloween Party

How many ghosts, skeletons, cats and pumpkins can you see at the Halloween party?

ANSWERS

1. Freaky Footprints

5.

2. Mumbo Jumbo

3.

3. Shadow Bats

4.

4. Crossroads

Highlands

5. Speedboat

Skier number 3

6. Jaws

Shark number 3

7. Haunted House

8. Mystery Tour

9. Spider's Web

2.

10. Snakes Alive

Snake number 2

11. Silly Sheep

16 sheep

12. Spot the Difference

13. Bungee Monkey

Monkey number 2

14. Mosquito Match

Mosquito numbers
2 and 5

15. Goo Who?

Number 4

16. Alien Eyeballs

There are three eyeballs

17. Secret code

You
have
cracked
the
secret
code

18. Snowbody There

19. Cat Splat

Shadow number 5

20. Witches' Hats

21. Top Secret

Use this code to write
other messages

22. Mummy Mummy!

Mummies number
1 and 6

23. Bubble Trouble

Number 4,
the lion

24. Laughing Hyenas

11 Hyenas

25. Blackout!

15 animals

26. Howl at the Moon

Pictures 3 and 6 match

27. Bugs!

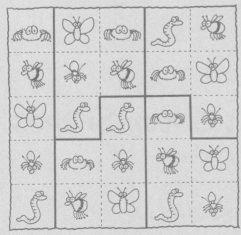

28. Mad Mars

10 Martians

29. Wizard!

30. Crazy Castle

Road A

31. Computer Connection

Controller A

32. Nine Dots

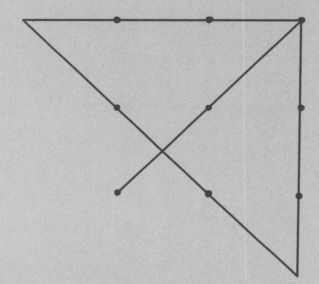

33. Over the Waves

34. Under the Sea

35. River Rapids

River B

36. Sailing Boat

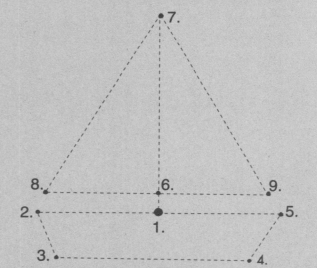

1–2–3–4–5–1–6–7–8–9–7

37. Clown Shapes

12 circles
4 triangles
14 squares

38. Envelope

1–2–3–4–5–6–4–1–3–6–2

39. Manic Monkeys

14 monkeys

40. Space Rocket

Rockets 4 and 6

41. Robot Shapes

10 circles
4 rectangles
3 triangles
3 squares

42. Sweet Boxes

43. Shadow Match

44. Strawberry Patch

22 strawberries

45. Dog and Bone

Route 1

46. Teddy's Bedroom

47. Snowman

Snowman number 4

48. Cake Puzzle

49. Flight of Fright

50. Fit for a King

51. Top Secret

Key 3

52. Treasure Trail

53. Splish Splat!

Splish Splats 3 and 4

54. Smiling Faces

55. High-five Spider

56. Bats' castle
18 bats

57. Star Gazing
32 stars

58. Alien Adventure
Route Z

59. Blast off

60. Kick It

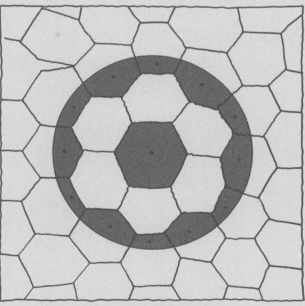

61. Cat Calling
The gerbil

62. Oodles of Doodles

Doodles 1 and 5

63. Jungle Trap

64. Sun, Moon and Stars

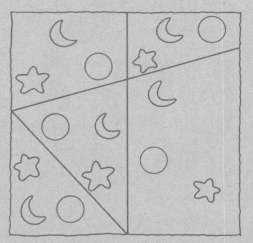

65. Zippy the Snail

Route C

66. Cat Nap

14 cats napping

67. Wibbly Wobbly

Wibbly wobbly men 4 and 6

68. Walkies

69. Home Sweet Home

70. Shadow Shark
Shadow 4

71. Beware of the Werewolf
Shadow 4

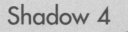

72. Splatman
Shadow 3

73. Maze Race

74. Sneaky Sandwich
Trail C, lobster

75. Shadow Match

76. Fast Fly
Route 1

77. Growly Grizzly
Growly grizzly number 1

78. Oops!

79. Farm Fun
20 animals

80. Wrong Way
Cat 2   Fish 4
Worm 5   Chicken 1

81. Teddy Bears
18 teddy bears

82. Snowflakes
Pictures 1 and 6

83. Fruity Split

84. Squeaky Floorboards

85. Vulture Trouble
Vulture 4

86. Kitty Tree
14 cats

87. Ancient Book
puzzle
books
are
great

88. Busy Bees

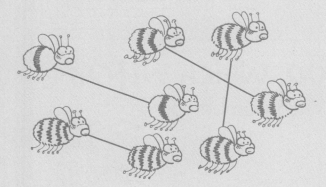

89. Squid's Hid

90. Rocket Science
Cord 1

91. Bathtime Tiger

92. Private Detective
Trail 2

93. Find the Fairies

94. Lion Match

Lions 3 and 5

95. Gift Box

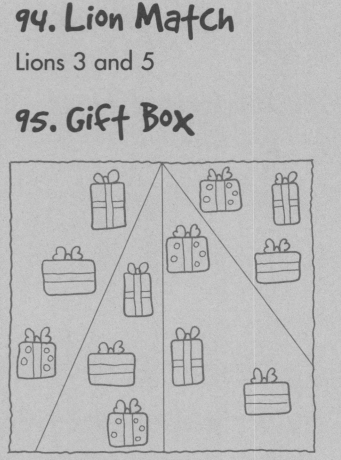

96. Zany Zebra

16 zebras

97. Duck!

Pond A has 20 ducks but pond B has 21.

98. Lovely Leaves

99. Secret Agent

100. Which Witch?

Witch number 5

101. Halloween Party

11 ghosts
4 skeletons
8 pumpkins
2 cats

Brainbender Puzzles

1. Paintbrush Puzzle

There are eight triangles in this six-pointed star. Move two brushes to make another six-pointed star, but with only six visible triangles.

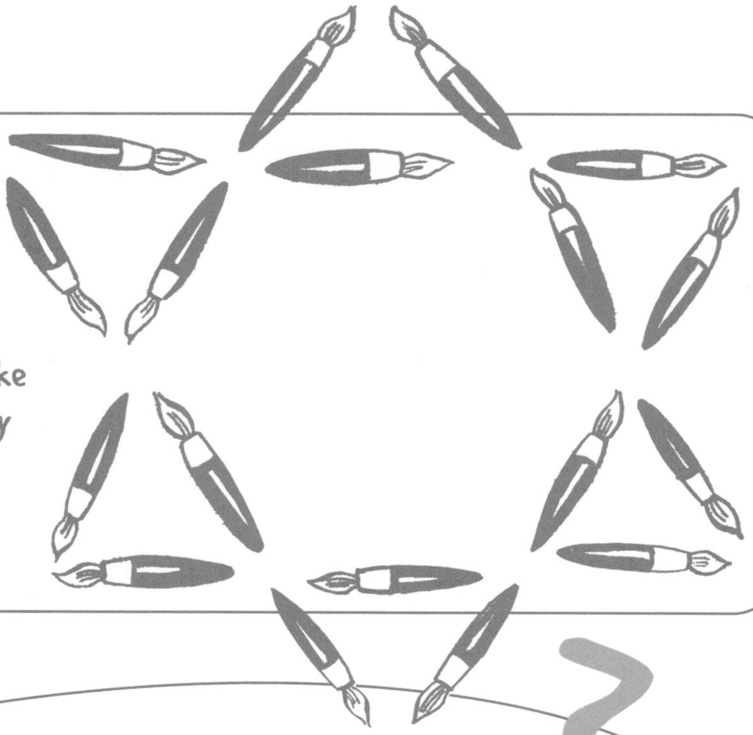

2. Logic Puzzler

What is it about you that changes every year, always going up and never coming down?

3. Anagram Antics

Unscramble each of these words to find something in the picture.

CORS SISS
HARM ME
ROT RAP
TO CORD

4. Number Search

Two numbers between one and twenty are missing from the box. Can you find them?

5. Baffling Bet

A man was sitting in a café enjoying a drink when the waiter came over to him and said "I'll bet you $2 that if you give me $2, I will give you $3 in return." The man was puzzled as he thought about it. Should he accept the bet or not?

6. Word Play

Look at the clues and see if you can make new words by changing just one letter in each of these words.

Change FORK to a kind of meat.
Change SHOW to the opposite of fast.
Change HARD to a thick type of paper.

7. Age Question

When asked how old she was, Rosie replied "In two years I will be twice as old as I was five years ago." How old is she?

8. Number Cross

Fill in the numbers in the number grid by solving the clues.

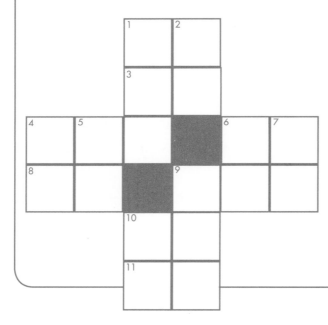

Across

1. Number of days in three weeks.
3. Six times seven.
4. 888 divided by four.
6. Half of seventy-six.
8. Four times seventeen.
9. Seven down plus eleven across.
10. 125 divided by five.
11. Eight + fourteen + eighteen.

Down

1. 121 doubled.
2. Thirty-six divided by three.
4. Half of fifty-two.
5. Eight across minus eleven across.
6. Four times eight.
7. Three across plus six across.
9. Half of 300.
10. Number of hours in a day.

9. Driving Dilemma

Bill was sitting in his car on an ordinary road pointing north. He turns to his friend and says "Even though we are pointing north, I can drive this car for one mile and end up one mile south of where we started from." How?

M	D	Y	T	A	F	W	U	Q	D	J	P
K	O	I	R	C	E	S	H	O	Z	K	S
T	B	U	J	O	C	I	G	L	B	D	Y
A	Z	Y	S	K	V	S	O	B	C	W	E
O	A	C	N	E	C	E	X	Y	I	N	K
G	I	P	L	K	F	S	N	A	C	R	N
F	O	S	J	F	T	D	D	O	F	L	O
H	R	C	A	W	I	B	K	S	I	Q	M
I	P	R	Q	U	X	N	T	H	P	L	X
K	I	Y	T	E	R	E	S	R	O	H	A
G	T	D	A	Z	C	I	O	J	U	C	B
R	W	A	C	F	L	X	B	D	R	I	B

10. Wild Wordsearch

Find these ten animals in the wordsearch.

GIRAFFE	HORSE
CAT	PIG
DOG	MONKEY
MOUSE	BIRD
LION	GOAT

11. Letter Change

Turn REAL into BELT by changing one letter at a time by following the clues.

1. Cotton and films come on this.
2. Sense of touch.
3. You walk on these.
4. A sort of pen tip.

REAL

_ _ _ _

_ _ _ _

_ _ _ _

_ _ _ _

BELT

12. Number Sequence

What's the next number in the sequence?

11 10 8 7 13 5

13. Ridiculous Riddle

Which source of heat is black when you buy it, red when you use it and gray when you throw it away?

14. Alphabet Puzzle

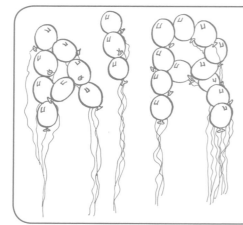

Put a different letter or letters in front of the word AIR each time to solve the clues.

1. Strands of this are on your head.   _AIR

2. At this you can go on different rides.   _AIR

3. You sit on this.   _AIR

15. Letter Assembler

Rearrange these letters to make a ten-letter word meaning "all."

THIEVE GRYN

16. What Am I?

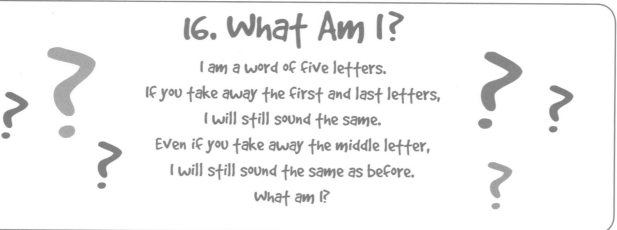

I am a word of five letters.
If you take away the first and last letters,
I will still sound the same.
Even if you take away the middle letter,
I will still sound the same as before.
What am I?

17. Mix And Match

Put the words below into their correct pairs.

Swan	Foal
Bear	Chick
Cow	Cygnet
Kangaroo	Cub
Rooster	Joey
Horse	Calf

18. Spot The Difference

Study the picture carefully for one minute. Then turn over the page and look at the same picture. Spot five things which are missing from the picture.

1. _____
2. _____
3. _____
4. _____
5. _____

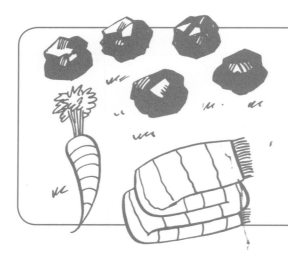

19. Solve The Mystery

It's the middle of winter and five pieces of coal, a carrot, and a scarf are lying on the lawn. Nobody put them there but there is a perfectly good explanation why they are there. What is it?

20. Word Change

Look at the clues and make new words by changing just one letter in each of these words:

1. Change TALK into a story.
2. Change GATE into something found on a calendar.
3. Change FINE into a number.

21. Proverb Puzzler

Rearrange the letters to form a well-known six-word saying. As in the question, there are six letters in the first word of the answer, five letters in the second, three letters in the third, four letters in the fourth, two letters in the fifth, and three letters in the sixth.

TRIKES HILWE ETH RONI SI THO

22. Number Cruncher

The number FIVE as written using block capitals contains exactly ten strokes or segments of a straight line. Can you find a number which, when written out as words, contains as many strokes as the number says. (Clue: it's between twenty and thirty.)

23. Word Wizz

Name the flowers that can be found by removing one letter from each word.

1. IRISH 2. ROUSE
3. MASTER 4. VIOLENT

24. Pencil Trick

Remove three pencils to leave three equal touching squares.

25. Letter Logic

What are the next four letters in the series? (Clue: there are twelve every year.)

J F M A M J J A

26. Countdown Conundrum

Seven men arrive at a meeting and each one shakes hands with all of the others. How many handshakes does that make?

27. Hidden Countries

In each of the sentences below, the name of a country is hidden. For example, the sentence: "Interpol and the FBI catch criminals" contains the word Poland. Can you find them?

1. Our dog likes his food so much he eats a can a day.
2. Always use a pencil when drawing lines in diagrams.
3. The king was angry when a thief stole his painting.
4. Does the teacher teach in a classroom?
5. In anger, many people say things they don't mean.

28. Adder

Answer the clues, then create a new word by joining the two answers together. Can you think of any other words that are made up in this way?

NOISE OF A COW
+ DANGER COLOR

= SECURED LIKE A BOAT

29. Tricky Words

Which word can be put before all the words below to make four new words?

FAST THROUGH DOWN AWAY

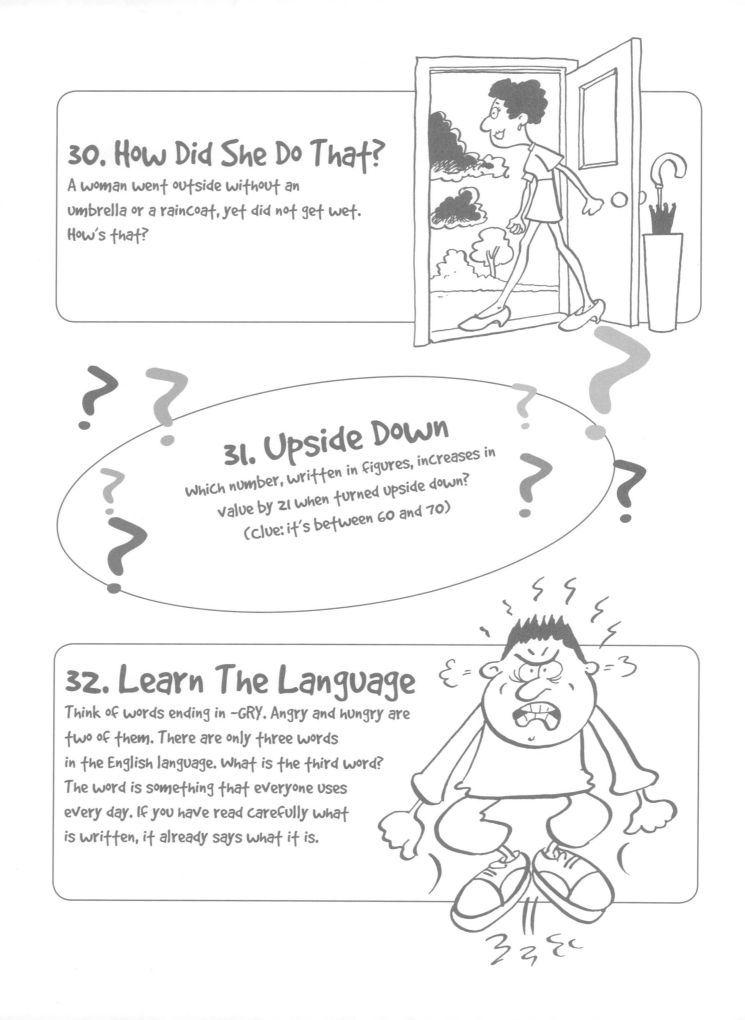

30. How Did She Do That?

A woman went outside without an umbrella or a raincoat, yet did not get wet. How's that?

31. Upside Down

Which number, written in figures, increases in value by 21 when turned upside down? (clue: it's between 60 and 70)

32. Learn The Language

Think of words ending in –GRY. Angry and hungry are two of them. There are only three words in the English language. What is the third word? The word is something that everyone uses every day. If you have read carefully what is written, it already says what it is.

33. Match Them Up
Match up the pairs.

34. Mind The Gap
Which single three-letter word completes all of the following words?

_ _ _ WARD

BE _ _ _ E

_ _ _ GED

IN_ _ _ MATION

35. Oddly Enough
What is the opposite of NOT OUT?

36. Figure It Out

Andy bought a bag of apples on Monday and ate a third of them. On Tuesday he ate half of the remaining apples. On Wednesday he looked in the bag to find he only had two apples left. How many apples were originally in the bag?

37. Date Dilemma

How many days is it from Wednesday August 1st to the first Saturday in September?

38. Missing Alphabet

Find the two letters missing from the ball.

39. Catch A Cat

If six cats can catch six rats in six minutes, how many cats are needed to catch ten rats in ten minutes?

40. Deadly Decision

An explorer is caught stealing food by a tribe who order that he must die. But the tribe chief is a reasonable man and allows the explorer to choose the method by which he will be killed. The explorer is asked to make a single statement. If it is true he will be thrown off a high cliff. If it is false he will be eaten by lions. What clever statement does the explorer make that forces the chief to let him go?

41. Animal Madness

Can you name the creature missing from the nursery rhyme?

1. Mary had a little ____.

2. With a nicknack paddywhack, give the ___ a bone.

3. Pop goes the _____.

4. The ___ jumped over the moon.

42. Wise Words

What is the one thing that all people, no matter how important they are, agree is between heaven and Earth?

43. Gambling Games

Tom and Nancy are playing a game of cards for $1 a game. At the end of the evening, Tom has won three games and Nancy has won $3. How many games did they play?

44. Put Them Together

Match up these characters with their other halves.

Gretel   Jane   Hermione Granger   Gandalf   Jerry

Harry Potter   Bilbo Baggins   Tom   Tarzan   Hansel

45. About Turn

A group of soldiers were standing in the boiling hot sun, facing west. Their sergeant shouted at them: "Right Turn! About Turn! Left Turn!" What direction are they now facing? Right and left turns are both 90 degrees, and an about turn is 180 degrees.

46. Complete The Sequence

What's the next letter in the list?

M T W T

47. Car Trouble

A four-wheeled car has traveled 24,000 miles and uses four tires. Each tire traveled the same distance. How far has each separate tire traveled?

48. Wacky Wordsearch

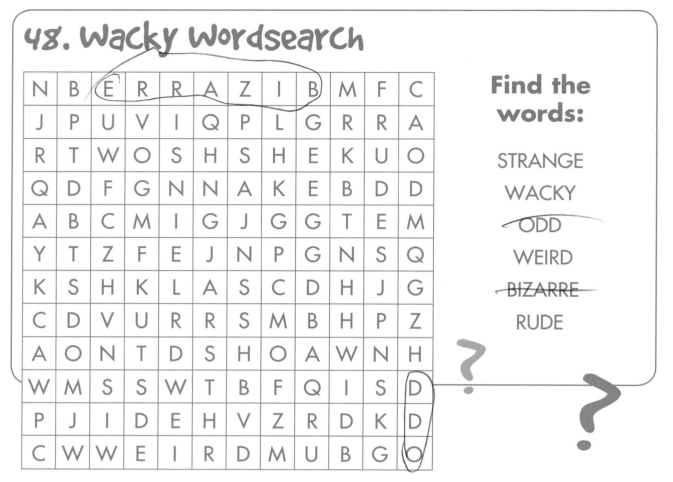

N	B	E	R	R	A	Z	I	B	M	F	C
J	P	U	V	I	Q	P	L	G	R	R	A
R	T	W	O	S	H	S	H	E	K	U	O
Q	D	F	G	N	N	A	K	E	B	D	D
A	B	C	M	I	G	J	G	G	T	E	M
Y	T	Z	F	E	J	N	P	G	N	S	Q
K	S	H	K	L	A	S	C	D	H	J	G
C	D	V	U	R	R	S	M	B	H	P	Z
A	O	N	T	D	S	H	O	A	W	N	H
W	M	S	S	W	T	B	F	Q	I	S	D
P	J	I	D	E	H	V	Z	R	D	K	D
C	W	W	E	I	R	D	M	U	B	G	O

Find the words:

STRANGE
WACKY
~~ODD~~
WEIRD
~~BIZARRE~~
RUDE

49. Number Solver

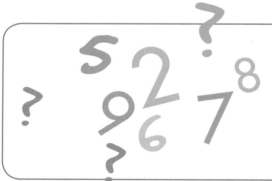

Find two whole numbers which, when multiplied together, give an answer of 61.

50. What Am I?

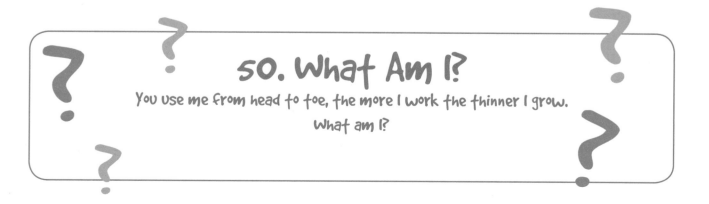

You use me from head to toe, the more I work the thinner I grow.
What am I?

51. Letter Game

HAND

- - - -

- - - -

- - - -

- - - -

FEET

Go from HAND to FEET by changing only one letter at a time.

1. This is found on a beach.
2. You do this to a letter.
3. You plant this to make a flower grow.
4. To take food in.

52. Picture Puzzle

Work out the saying from the picture.

ARREST

YOU'RE

53. Pencil Palaver

Take away six pencils to leave three equal-sized squares.

54. Sweet Tooth

Five children were sharing out a box of sweets. Bob took five, Peter took five, Joey took five, and Danny took five. That left half the pack, which Natasha took. How many sweets were there altogether?

FLUFF
IRAQI
ROBIN
SANTA
TOTAL

55. Long List

What's special about the list of words opposite? (Clue: look at the beginning and end of each word.)

56. Number Parts

Bill's number is two, Clare's number is three, and Edward's number is five. What is Donna's number?

57. Body Parts

Name ten body parts that are spelt with three letters. No slang words!

58. Pictionary

Work out the saying from the picture.

59. Chocolate Challenge

One boy can eat sixteen chocolates in half a minute, and another can eat half as many in twice the length of time. How many chocolates can both boys eat between them in fifteen seconds?

60. Common Factor

What letter do the following numbers have in common?

3, 7, 10, 11, 12

61. Sleep Tight

Turn the word SLEEP into DREAM by changing one letter at a time.

1. An alarm clock makes this noise.
2. What happens when you cut yourself.
3. A species of something.
4. Eat this with peanut butter.
5. Not looking forward to something.

SLEEP

_ _ _ _ _

_ _ _ _ _

_ _ _ _ _

_ _ _ _ _

_ _ _ _ _

DREAM

62. Sink or Swim

Reposition three pencils to make the fish swim in the opposite direction.

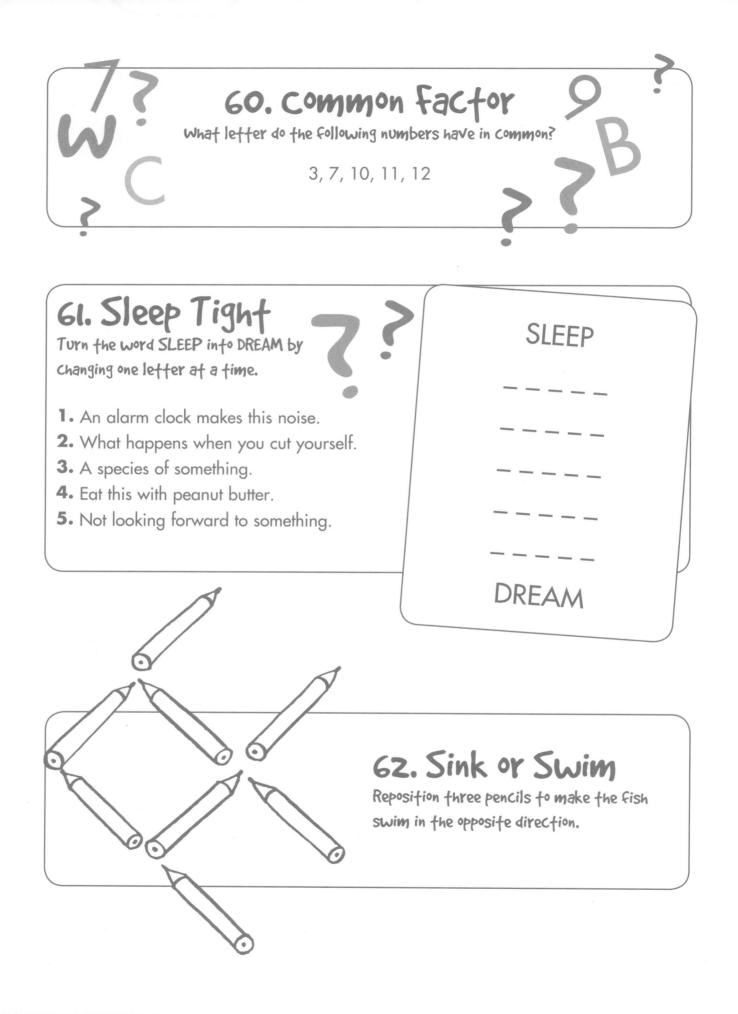

63. Picture Guess

Discover the saying from the picture.

64. Memory Trick

Pick a number between one and ten. Multiply by nine. Subtract five. Add the digits together and repeat this step until you have a one-digit number. For whatever number you have, pick that letter of the alphabet. E.g. A = 1, B = 2, etc.

Now think of a country beginning with that letter.

Think of an animal that begins with the second letter of the country.

Think of a color usually associated with the animal. What do you have?

65. A Dog's Life

Once there was a dog named Nelly, who lived on a farm. There were three other dogs on the farm. Their names were Blackie, Whitey, and Brownie. What do you think the fourth dog's name was?

66. Anagram Anger

Rearrange these letters to give the title of a famous wizard.

PORT TRAY HER

67. Memorize This

Look at the picture below for one minute. Then cover it up (no cheating!) and answer the questions.

1. How many loaves of bread are there in the bakery window?
2. Whose bakery is it?
3. What hairstyles do the twins have?
4. What time is it?
5. Is the toy store closed or open?

68. Odd One Out

Which of the following words doesn't belong in the group and why?

LAME   MALE   MEAL   MEAT

69. Building Split

This row of ten letters can be split into two five-letter words which are the names of two things used to make buildings. Words read from left to right and the letters are in the correct order. What are they?

B R S I T O C K N E

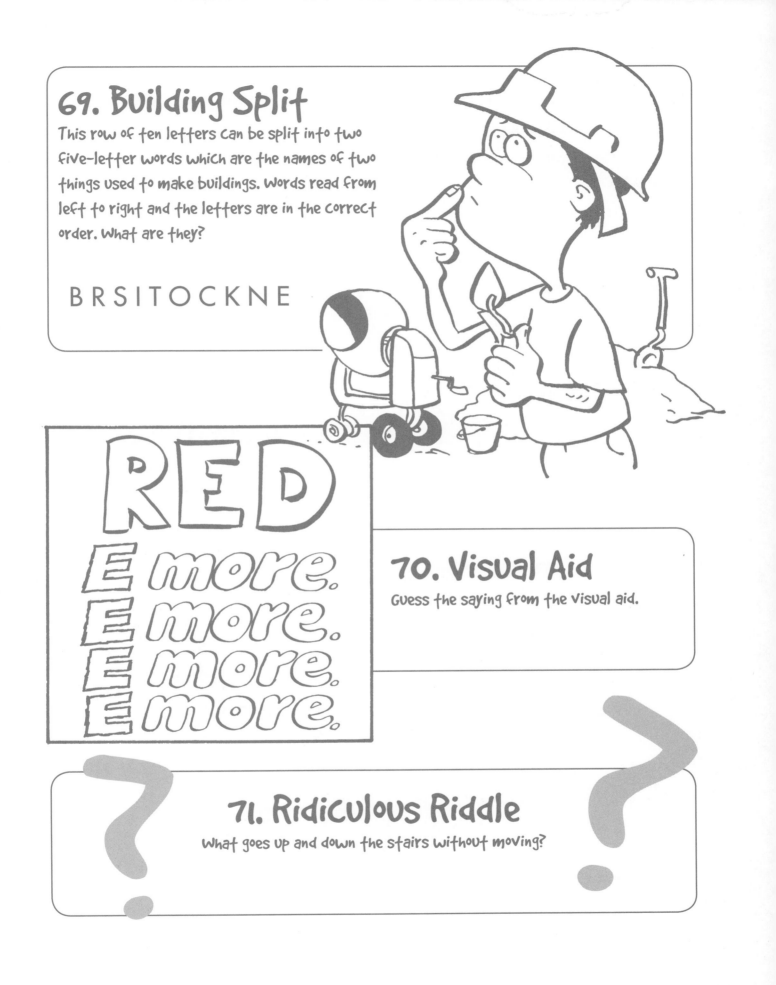

RED
E more.
E more.
E more.
E more.

70. Visual Aid

Guess the saying from the visual aid.

71. Ridiculous Riddle

What goes up and down the stairs without moving?

72. Snakes Alive

The name of a type of snake is hidden in each of the sentences below. Find them by joining words or parts of words together.

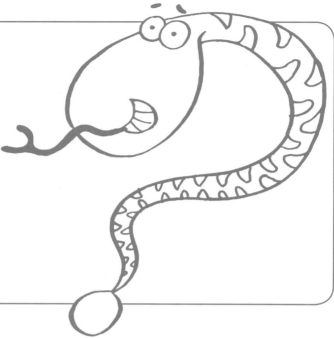

1. How sad Derek looks.
2. They stayed all night at the disco, bravely in my opinion.
3. The jumbo arrived on time.

73. Flower Power

Here are the names of four flowers with the vowels removed. Can you name them?

DSY   BTTRCP   DFFDL   SNFLWR

74. Hunt The Word

The letters missing from this box make up the name of an animal. Can you name it?

75. Happy Birthday

Sally was eight the day before yesterday.

Next year she will be ten.

What is the date of Sally's birthday, and on which date would the first two things have been true?

76. Tennis Trouble

Two men were playing tennis. They played five sets and each man won three sets. How can this be possible?

77. Spoon Puzzle

Reposition six of the spoons in the pattern below to make six equal-sized diamond shapes in a star pattern.

78. What's Next?
What's the next letter in the series?

B, C, D, E, G

79. What Is It?
Guess the phrase from the picture.

Me right

80. Tall Tale
Before Mount Everest was discovered, what was the tallest mountain in the world?

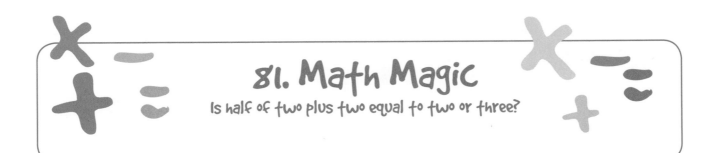

81. Math Magic
Is half of two plus two equal to two or three?

82. Give Me Five

Solve the clues, so that each answer contains five letters. Write all the answers in place and the shaded squares reading down will reveal the name of a musical instrument.

1. Opposite of last.
2. Outer covering of an egg.
3. Sail boat.
4. Bad weather.
5. The Human _ _ _ _ _.
6. Push this to power a bicycle.
7. Meadow.
8. Number in a trio.

1. _ _ _ _ _
2. _ _ _ _ _
3. _ _ _ _ _
4. _ _ _ _ _
5. _ _ _ _ _
6. _ _ _ _ _
7. _ _ _ _ _
8. _ _ _ _ _

83. Word Mix
Rearrange the letters of GROW NO LINSEED to spell one single word.

GROW NO
LINSEED

84. Word Ladder

Change NOSE into FAST by changing one letter at a time.

1. Misplace.
2. Opposite of found.
3. At the back.

NOSE

_ _ _ _

_ _ _ _

_ _ _ _

FAST

85. Big Is Best

Who is bigger? Mr Bigger, Mrs Bigger, or their baby?

86. The Hole Truth

If it takes three people to dig a hole, how many people does it take to dig half a hole?

87. Math Equation

If five thousand, five hundred and five dollars is written as $5,505, how should twelve thousand, twelve hundred and twelve dollars be written?

88. Matchstick Marvel

Reposition four matches from this pattern to form five triangles.

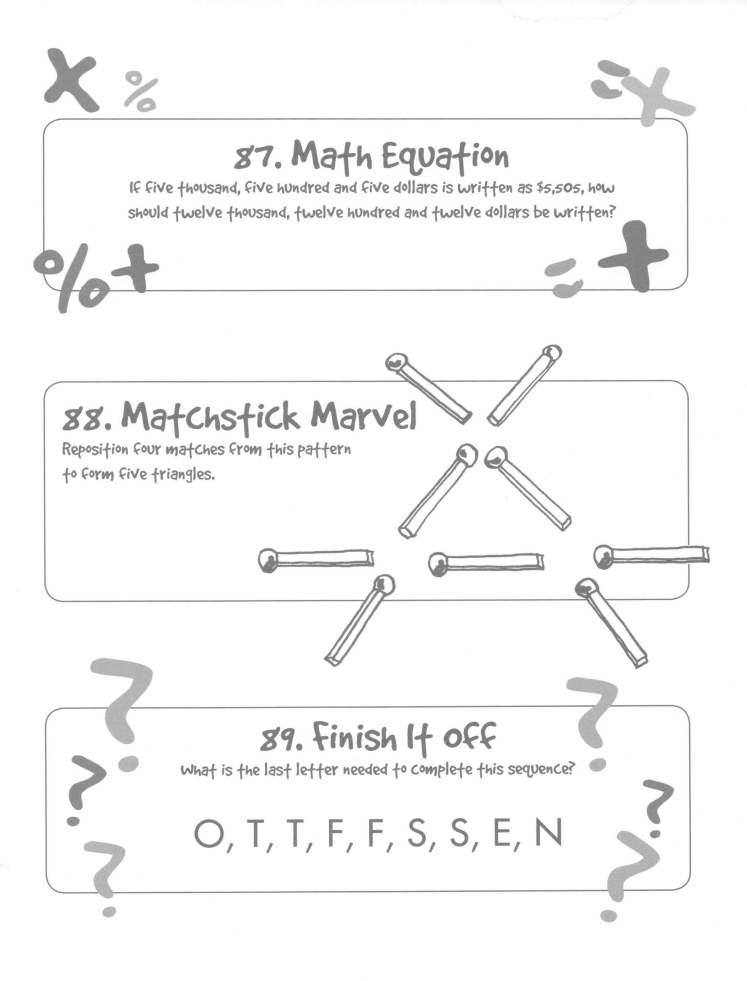

89. Finish It Off

What is the last letter needed to complete this sequence?

O, T, T, F, F, S, S, E, N

90. How Confusing

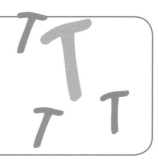

What starts with a T, ends with a T
and has T in it?

91. What Am I?

My first is in Chair
But isn't in Chain

My second is in pale
And also in pain

My third is in edge
But isn't in green

My fourth is in lime
But isn't in mean

My fifth's in Cone
And also in round.

Do you know what I am?
I'm connected with sound!

92. Hot or Cold?

What moves faster,
heat or cold?

~~cold~~

Heat

93. Math Trick

When can you add two to eleven and get one?

94. Word Scramble

Rearrange these letters to give the names of some
animals you might find at the zoo.

DANAP

KNOMEY

NAHPETLE

FEIRAGF

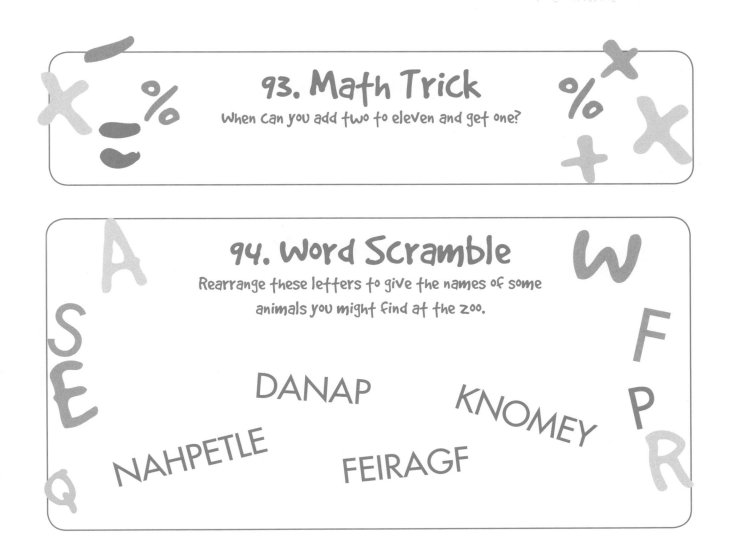

95. Work It Out

If two hours ago, it was exactly as long after one o'clock in the afternoon as it was
before one o'clock in the morning, what time would it be now?

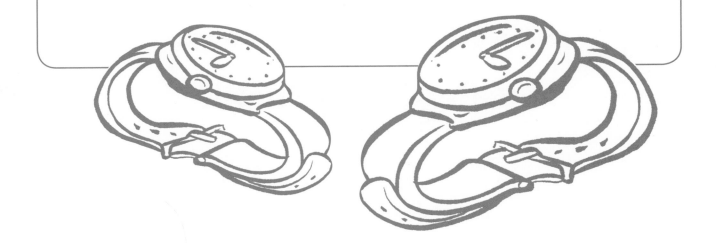

96. Animal Tracks

Make tracks and find seven different animals in the grid. Start at the letter in the top left square and move in any direction except diagonally. Every letter is used once.

C A M E A R
L L E B E L E
I A R D E P
O P E G H
N O R E T A
L E A P T N

97. Take Away

What is it that, when you take away the whole, you still have some left over?

98. Perplexing Puzzle

What is in the middle of nowhere?

99. Bowling

Four friends go bowling together. They decide that they will each play each other once.
How many games will they play?

four

100. Fitting In

What is the only other letter that fits in the following series?

B, C, D, E, I, K, O, X

101. Key Words

There's a problem on the keyboard of Clare's computer. She types in letters but the screen only shows numbers! In each case the letter links to a number below it.

So, for example, 1 can stand for a Q, an A or a Z.

The number 9 could be an O or an L.

Can you work out what Clare was trying to say?

8 2165 5682 7136863
59 53 43018433

ANSWERS

1. Paintbrush Puzzle

2. Logic Puzzler

Your age.

3. Anagram Antics

Scissors
Hammer
Parrot
Doctor

4. Number Search

13 and 19

5. Baffling Bet

The man is in a no-win situation—even if he wins the bet he still loses $1 of his money.

6. Word Play

Pork
Slow
Card

7. Age Question

She's twelve.

8. Number Cross

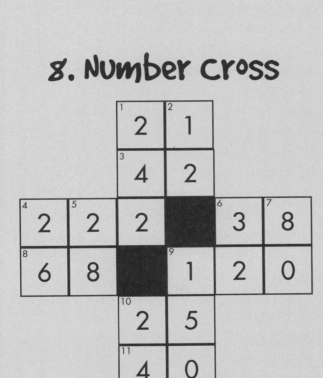

9. Driving Dilemma

Bill was driving in reverse.

10. Wild Wordsearch

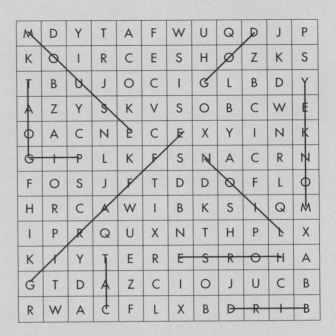

11. Letter Change

1. REEL
2. FEEL
3. FEET
4. FELT

12. Number Sequence

Fourteen—each time you add on two,
then one, then two, then one and so on.

13. Ridiculous Riddle

Coal

14. Alphabet Puzzle

1. Hair
2. Fair
3. Chair

15. Letter Assembler

Everything

16. What Am I?

Empty

17. Mix And Match

Swan + cygnet
Bear + cub
Cow + calf
Kangaroo + joey
Rooster + chick
Horse + foal

18. Spot The Difference

1. The bottle of drink has gone.
2. The woman's glasses have disappeared.
3. There are now only two balloons.
4. There are only four people queuing for ice cream now.
5. There are five birds in the air now.

19. Solve The Mystery

They were used to make a snowman. The snow has melted.

20. Word Change

1. Tale
2. Date
3. Nine or Five

21. Proverb Puzzler

Strike while the iron is hot

22. Number Cruncher

TWENTY NINE

23. Word Wizz

1. IRIS 2. ROSE
3. ASTER 4. VIOLET

24. Pencil Trick

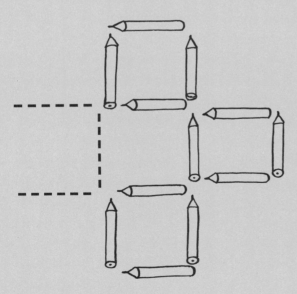

25. Letter Logic

S O N D—they are all the first
letters of months of the year

26. Countdown Conundrum

21

27. Hidden Countries

1. Canada—Our dog likes his food so
much he eats a **can a d**ay.
2. India—Always use a pencil when
drawing lines **in dia**grams.
3. Spain—The king was angry when a
thief stole hi**s pain**ting.
4. China—Does the teacher tea**ch in a**
classroom?
5. Germany—In an**ger, many** people
say things they don't mean.

28. Adder

Moored

29. Tricky Words

They can all have the word BREAK in
front of them to make a new word.

30. How Did She Do That?

It wasn't raining.

31. Upside Down

68 (changes to 89)

32. Learn The Language

The key sentences are: There are only three words in the English language. What is the third word? The third word is "language."

33. Match Them Up

34. Mind The Gap

For

35. Oddly Enough

Out!

36. Figure It Out

He had six apples to start with and ate two apples on the first day and two on the second.

37. Date Dilemma

32—including both dates.

38. Missing Alphabet

K and R

39. Catch A Cat

Six cats

40. Deadly Decision

The explorer makes the statement: "I will be killed by the lions." Now if the chief feeds him to the lions, his statement will be true, so he should be thrown off the cliff. But if he is thrown off the cliff, his statement will be false. The chief has to let the explorer go!

41. Animal Madness

1. Lamb
2. Dog
3. Weasel
4. Cow

42. Wise Words

AND is between heaven and Earth.

43. Gambling Games

They played nine games. Tom won three games and Nancy won six games.

44. Put Them Together

Hansel and Gretel
Tarzan and Jane
Harry Potter and Hermione Granger
Tom and Jerry
Bilbo Baggins and Gandalf

45. About Turn

East

46. Complete The Sequence

The next letter is F— the days of the week.

47. Car Trouble

They all traveled the same distance—24,000 miles each.

48. Wacky Wordsearch

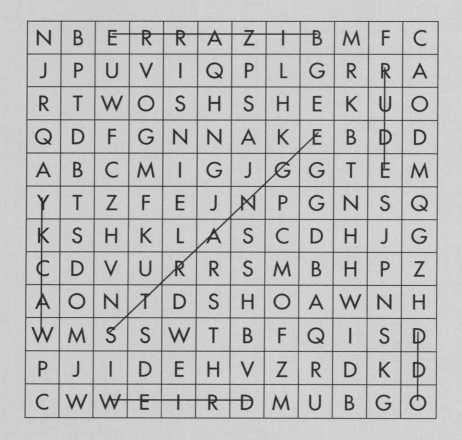

N	B	E	R	R	A	Z	I	B	M	F	C
J	P	U	V	I	Q	P	L	G	R	R	A
R	T	W	O	S	H	S	H	E	K	U	O
Q	D	F	G	N	N	A	K	E	B	D	D
A	B	C	M	I	G	J	G	G	T	E	M
Y	T	Z	F	E	J	N	P	G	N	S	Q
K	S	H	K	L	A	S	C	D	H	J	G
C	D	V	U	R	R	S	M	B	H	P	Z
A	O	N	T	D	S	H	O	A	W	N	H
W	M	S	S	W	T	B	F	Q	I	S	D
P	J	I	D	E	H	V	Z	R	D	K	D
C	W	W	E	I	R	D	M	U	B	G	O

49. Number Solver

1 x 61

50. What Am I?

A bar of soap.

51. Letter Game

1. Sand
2. Send
3. Seed
4. Feed

52. Picture Puzzle

You're under arrest.

53. Pencil Palaver

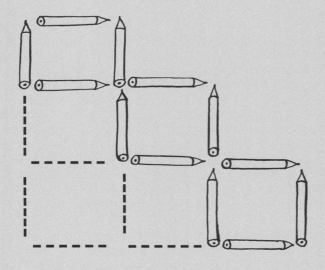

54. Sweet Tooth

40

55. Long List

The first letters in sequence, spell FIRST, the final letters spell FINAL.

56. Number Parts

Four—the first letter of the name has a value with A = 1, B = 2, etc.

57. Body Parts

Arm, Ear, Eye, Gum, Hip, Jaw, Lip, Leg, Rib, Toe. Not: Bum, Gut, Lap!

58. Pictionary

Time after time

59. Chocolate Challenge

Ten chocolates

60. Common Factor

The only vowel they contain when written out fully is the letter E.

61. Sleep Tight

1. Bleep
2. Bleed
3. Breed
4. Bread
5. Dread

62. Sink or Swim

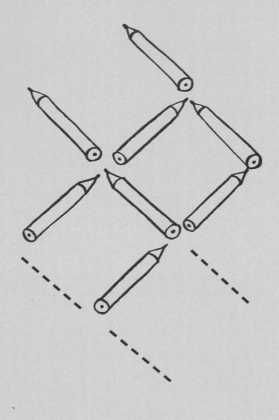

63. Picture Guess

Missing the letters used to spell "Link."

64. Memory Trick

Do you have a gray elephant from Denmark? Now try it on your friends!

65. A Dog's Life

Nelly

66. Anagram Anger

Harry Potter

67. Memorize This

1. Four
2. Bernie's
3. Plaits
4. 10.30 am
5. Open

68. Odd One Out

Meat—all the others are anagrams of each other.

69. Building Split

Brick and Stone

70. Visual Aid

Ready for more.

71. Ridiculous Riddle

A carpet

72. Snakes Alive

1. Adder
2. Cobra
3. Boa

73. Flower Power

1. Daisy
2. Buttercup
3. Daffodil
4. Sunflower

74. Hunt The Word

Bear

75. Happy Birthday

Sally's birthday is December 31. The information would have been true on January 1.

76. Tennis Trouble

The two men were partners playing doubles.

77. Spoon Puzzle

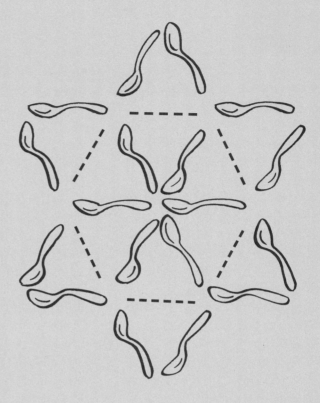

78. What's Next?

P—they all rhyme.

79. What Is It?

Right beside me

80. Tall Tale

Mount Everest—it was the tallest mountain even before it was discovered!

81. Math Magic

Three

82. Give Me Five

1. First
2. Shell
3. Yacht
4. Storm
5. Torch
6. Pedal
7. Field
8. Three

The musical instrument made
is a RECORDER

83. Word Mix

ONE SINGLE WORD

84. Word Ladder

1. Lose
2. Lost
3. Last

85. Big Is Best

The baby, because he's a
little bigger!

86. The Hole Truth

You can't dig half a hole!

87. Math Equation

$13,212

88. Matchstick Marvel

89. Finish It Off

T—the letters are the initials of the numbers one to ten.

90. How Confusing

A teapot

91. What Am I?

Radio

92. Hot or Cold

Heat—everyone can catch a cold!

93. Math Trick

When you add two hours to eleven o'clock you get one o'clock.

94. Word Scramble

Elephant
Panda
Giraffe
Monkey

95. Work It Out

Nine o'clock—since there are twelve hours between the two times, and half of that time equals six, then the halfway mark would have to be seven o'clock.
If it were seven o'clock, two hours ago, then the time would now be nine o'clock.

96. Animal Tracks

1. Camel
2. Lion
3. Leopard
4. Bear
5. Elephant
6. Tiger
7. Ape

97. Take Away

The word "wholesome."

98. Perplexing Puzzle

The Letter "H."

99. Bowling

There are six games.

100. Fitting In

H—all of the letters in the series flipped vertically look the same.

101. Key Words

I WANT THIS
MACHINE TO
BE REPAIRED.